THIS MYSTART JOURNAL BELONGS TO

MYSTART
JOURNAL

---

www.mystartjournal.com

DEDICATION

The Mystart Journal is dedicated to:
William V "Quint", Tobias, Jadyn, Caleb, Ethan, Isabel, Hannah,
Caleb, Silas, Ella
and
all the special kids who are in our lives.
We can think of nothing sweeter to pass on to you than our love
for God's word and hearing the Holy Spirit's gentle voice.
Our prayer is that your hearts will always
make room for Jesus.

"My son, incline your ear to my sayings…for they are life to those
who find them."
(Prov. 4:20, 22)

CONTENTS

HEY KIDS, WELCOME TO YOUR NEW JOURNAL

Welcome to your MYSTART Journal

This journal is being used by kids all over the world who want to read the Bible and hear what God is saying to them through His word.

MYSTART Journal

4 Quarters
4 Themes
1 Journal entry a week
We'll travel through four major themes: Identity, Character, Adventure and Trust, spending 12 weeks on each theme and then there's space for you to reflect on your journey and do a HEART CHECKUP.

All Scriptures are taken from the NIRV Holy Bible, New International Reader's Version®, NIrV® Copyright © 1995, 1996, 1998, 2014.

Join our Online Community

Sharing your adventures is always fun! We've created an online community where you get updates, share your experiences and connect with kids from around the world.
Are you ready for the fun to begin?

LET'S START THE ADVENTURE

How It All Works
You will need about 15-20 minutes to complete your Lectio Divina.

S – Scripture
Write out the part of the scripture that stands out to you?
It might be a phrase or a line or even just a word.

T – Think
Think about what the Scripture is saying.
How does this relate to you right now?

A – Ask
Write out a prayer.
As you look at what God is saying to you, write a prayer about what He is showing you through the scripture.

R – Rest
Set your stopwatch for at least 2-5 minutes.
Listen for God's still small voice (in your mind) reminding you of who He is. Finish this sentence, "God is my _____ ". When your mind wants to wander, come back to this thought you have about God.

T – Tell
Tell an adult in your life what God has told you OR jump online to mystartjournal.com and let us know what you learned during the Lectio Divina.

MEET YOUR COACH

I'm Miss Penny and I'll be your coach as you go through this journey.

Check out the fun facts.

Name: Miss Penny
Age: (I'll never tell ...)
Job: Kids Pastor
Drink: Peach Ice Tea
Ice Cream: Cookies 'n Cream
Dessert: Chocolate Cake
Flower: Sunflower
Hobbies: Reading, playing basketball and guitar
Bible Verse: Jeremiah 29:11
Color: Green
Pet: Millie the cat

FAQ's

What does "Lectio Divina" mean?
Lectio Divina means divine reading. Since the early days of the Church, the Lectio has been used as a method to interact and engage with the scriptures. God's Word is living and active and sharper than any two-edged sword (Hebrews 4:12) and instructs our hearts in His way. A Lectio gives us the space, time and structure to make that possible.

What makes a Lectio Divina different from other types of journaling?
The Lectio Divina is all about LISTENING. Between each of the START segments, you read the scripture again SLOWLY... VERY SLOWLY... and if you can, read it out aloud. LISTEN for God's voice as you read it. An important part of a Lectio Divina, is the REST time. Some adults rest for up to 20 minutes. Some kids set their stopwatch for 5 minutes. Some groups decide to say, "The Lord's Prayer" together and then begin the REST time. How long you rest is up to you. You might start at a couple of minutes and increase your time. Have fun with it.

How can the MYSTART Journal be used in a group?
Lectios are used by individuals or in a group setting. Some ideas for using the journal in a group:
- Take turns reading the scripture before each section of the MYSTART Journal.
- Say the Lord's prayer together before the REST time.
- Enjoy sharing journal entries together at the end of the Lectio.

IDENTITY

MY LIFE

Penny's Short Stories - IDENTITY

"The Incredibles" is one of my favorite Disney Pixar movies. The story is of a family of superheroes who conceal their true identity and try to pretend to be normal people until their cover is blown and they get mixed up in a plot to overtake the world. The superheroes find it very difficult to pretend to be someone they aren't. Lots of people spend their lives trying to find out who they really are. They pretend their way through their lives and miss out on the purpose they were created for. This quarter we are looking at Identity, discovering who we are and why God created us. Check out this journal entry by Mandy.

Hey there,

I'm Mandy.

I'm in Grade 5 and I love playing soccer. My dad is my coach and we train really hard. I hope one day to make it into one of the big tournaments. Every night my dad and I train together after school and then once a week we get together with the other team members for our scheduled training session. I wear a number on my back, but I'm not known by that number. My friends call me Mandy when they pass me the ball. The opposition team doesn't know my name. So they will call out, "Mark #10!" to their team. They will try anything to block me scoring a goal.

Last week we played the Hornets. They're a tough team. Ten minutes into the second half, I was dribbling the ball up the field and was getting ready to shoot a goal, when the opposition tackled me and started calling me names and telling me what a terrible player I was. The words hurt me. Everything in me wanted to walk off the field and kiss the game goodbye. But, then I heard my dad calling out from the sideline, "Get back up. It's time for another goal.

Remember who you are and what team you belong to. You're Mandy and you're a goal scorer. Let's Go!". That's all I needed to hear. When I heard my dad on the sideline yelling out his encouragement to me, I got back up and with renewed determination scored a goal.

On the way home my dad and I were talking about the game and I was saying how much I hate it when the opposing team tries to get me angry by pushing my buttons and getting me off my game. I said to him, that if he hadn't encouraged me from the sideline, I might have quit.

Dad said it reminded him of a bigger battle that is happening. God calls us by name and we belong to his team, but to the enemy we are just a number. He taunts us and teases us, trying to distract us and get us away from our purpose. But if we know who we are and whose team we are on, we can keep going knowing there's a grandstand of people who have gone before us cheering us on like the Bible says in Hebrews 12.

I know that the opposing teams are not going to stop trying to distract me, but I have my dad's voice in my ears, "Remember who you are and what team you belong to."

Mandy

I love this story Mandy wrote in her journal. It reminded me that our Heavenly Father knows who we are: we belong to Him. We can know His voice and follow His advice. The Apostle Paul told us in Ephesians that it's in Christ that we find out who we are and what we are living for.

As Christians, we don't need to pretend or wonder who we are. When we follow Jesus we find out who we are and why we are on the planet.

IS THIS A DREAM?
Listening to God

A couple of years ago, I took a bunch of kids camping. I remember saying goodnight, checking on the cabins and all seemed quiet. I went to bed and fell asleep. I woke up a few hours later to the sound of voices outside my cabin. I peeked out of my cabin window and saw a bunch of kids running around in the dark. I got up and stood at my door, and after they saw me they hurried back to bed. I thought it was a dream, but it was real! Has anyone ever called out your name in the middle of the night when you were fast asleep? A bit scary, huh?

That happened to Samuel when he was a young boy living in the tabernacle with Eli, the priest. When he heard a voice call "Samuel...Samuel", he ran to ask Eli what he wanted. This happened three times, the first two times Eli told him he was not calling his name and to go back to bed. We will pick up the story on the third time when Eli realized God was calling Samuel. Samuel really trusted Eli, find out what happened next.

Scripture:
I Samuel 3:8-11
The Lord called out to Samuel for the third time. Samuel got up and went to Eli. He said, "Here I am. You called out to me." Then Eli realized that the Lord was calling the boy. So Eli told Samuel, "Go and lie down. If someone calls out to you again, say, 'Speak, Lord, I am listening." So Samuel went and lay down in his place. The Lord came and stood there. He called out, just as he had done the other times. He said, " Samuel! Samuel!" Then Samuel replied, "Speak. I'm listening." The Lord said to Samuel, "Pay attention!..."

S - Scripture (Read the scripture out loud slowly.)
Write the part of the scripture that stands out to you. It might be a phrase or a line or even just a word.

_____

T - Think (Read the scripture slowly again.)
Think about what the scripture is saying. How does this fit your life right now?

_____

_____

_____

_____

A - Ask (One more time...read the scripture slowly.)
Write a prayer about what God is showing you through the scripture.

_____

_____

_____

_____

 R - Rest (Set your stopwatch for at least 2 - 5 minutes.)
Listen for God's still small voice (in your mind) saying who He is.
Finish this sentence, "God is my _____."

 T - Tell
Tell an adult about what God has told you AND/OR you could jump online at mystartjournal.com and let us know what you learned today.

WHO AM I?
God has chosen us to be in His family

A few years ago I got a new kitten I called Henry. He was beautiful. A gorgeous ginger and white color. He had a lovely nature. We rescued him from the animal shelter and brought him into our family. We paid the adoption fee, signed the paperwork and from that day on, Henry belonged to us. When anyone asked us about him, we would say, "This is Henry, he has just joined our family." Henry was a nice cat, but before he was anything, he was OURS. That's how God feels about you.

Before you are anything, you are His special treasure. His amazing creation. And just like we adopted Henry, God has chosen you and adopted you as His. He paid the price to save you from your sins when he sent Jesus to die on the cross for you. He signed the paperwork that said your sins are forgiven and brought you into His family. God chose You. God loves you and He adopted you as His own kid because of all Jesus has done.

Don't take my word for it, check out the Apostle Paul's words in Ephesians as you journal today.

Scripture:
Ephesians 1:4-6
God chose us to belong to Christ before the world was created. He chose us to be holy and without blame in his eyes. He loved us. So he decided long ago to adopt us. He adopted us as his children with all the rights children have. He did it because of what Jesus Christ has done. It pleased God to do it.

S - Scripture (Read the scripture out loud slowly.)
Write the part of the scripture that stands out to you. It might be a phrase or a line or even just a word.

_____

T - Think (Read the scripture slowly again.)
Think about what the scripture is saying. How does this fit your life right now?

_____

_____

_____

_____

A - Ask (One more time...read the scripture slowly.)
Write a prayer about what God is showing you through the scripture.

_____

_____

_____

_____

R - Rest (Set your stopwatch for at least 2 - 5 minutes.)
Listen for God's still small voice (in your mind) saying who He is.
Finish this sentence, "God is my _____."

T - Tell
Tell an adult about what God has told you AND/OR you could jump online at mystartjournal.com and let us know what you learned today.

NOBODY CAN STEAL WHO YOU REALLY ARE
A focus on self-identity

A horrible thing happened to me last year. My credit card company called me and said my "identity" had been stolen and someone was using my credit card information for off-shore gambling! What? I don't gamble and I've never been in the Dominican Republic where this was taking place!

Thanks to the good people at VISA, they corrected it all, but it was a bit scary to think someone had my private information. Actually, that gambler did not steal my identity. He stole a credit card number and my identity is not about a plastic card.

Let's pretend you have a driver's license in your pocket. On it would be information about you. And if you put down your real age, it's obvious you would not be driving me to the market! So, let's just say you have a card that looks like a driver's license and it has on it words that tell who you really are, your "true identity".

As you begin to think about some of your descriptions, I have some great verses to help you. Read them slowly and circle the words that you feel God is speaking to you about your own identity. Then think about which word is the best one that describes who you really are.

Scripture:
Romans 8:14 - Those who are led by the Spirit of God are children of God.
2 Corinthians 5:17 - Anyone who believes in Christ is a new creation. The old is gone! The new has come!

John 15:15 - "I do not call you servants anymore. Servants do not know their master's business. Instead, I have called you friends. I have told you everything I learned from my Father.'"

S - Scripture (Read the scripture out loud slowly.)
Write the part of the scripture that stands out to you. It might be a phrase or a line or even just a word.

_____

T - Think (Read the scripture slowly again.)
Think about what the scripture is saying. How does this fit your life right now?

_____

_____

_____

_____

A - Ask (One more time…read the scripture slowly.)
Write a prayer about what God is showing you through the scripture.

_____

_____

_____

_____

R - Rest (Set your stopwatch for at least 2 - 5 minutes.)
Listen for God's still small voice (in your mind) saying who He is.
Finish this sentence, "God is my _____."

T - Tell
Tell an adult about what God has told you AND/OR you could jump online at mystartjournal.com and let us know what you learned today.

NO FAKES ALLOWED
Be yourself

Do you like to dress up? Each year in our Kids Ministry, we have a Pirates and Princess Party. The kids all come dressed up and have a lot of fun pretending to be someone else. Dress-up parties are fun, but they don't last forever. It's fun for a little while, but sooner or later, the outfit has to come off. The problem comes when we try to pretend to be someone that we aren't in normal life.

David knows how this feels. He was in the field tending sheep when his dad asked him to take lunch to his brothers. When David approached the battleground where his brothers were, he was surprised to see that no one was fighting the giant that was bullying the Israelites. David volunteered and offered to go out and fight the giant. King Saul decided to dress David up in his armor, but it didn't fit him, so he had to take it off.

God has made you unique. You don't have to be anyone else. No fakes allowed. Wear the clothes God has picked out for you and don't try to be someone else.

Let's learn from David's story...

Scripture:
1 Samuel 17:38-40
Then Saul dressed David in his own military clothes. He put a coat of armor on him. He put a bronze helmet on his head. David put on Saul's sword over his clothes. He walked around for awhile in all that armor because he wasn't used to it. "I can't go out there in all this armor," he said to Saul. "I'm not used to it." So he took it off. Then David picked up his wooden staff. He went down to a stream and chose five smooth stones. He put them in the pocket of his shepherd's bag. Then he took his sling in his hand and approached Goliath.

S - Scripture (Read the scripture out loud slowly.)
Write the part of the scripture that stands out to you. It might be a phrase or a line or even just a word.

_____

T - Think (Read the scripture slowly again.)
Think about what the scripture is saying. How does this fit your life right now?

_____

_____

_____

_____

A - Ask (One more time...read the scripture slowly.)
Write a prayer about what God is showing you through the scripture.

_____

_____

_____

_____

R - Rest (Set your stopwatch for at least 2 - 5 minutes.)
Listen for God's still small voice (in your mind) saying who He is.
Finish this sentence, "God is my _____."

T - Tell
Tell an adult about what God has told you AND/OR you could jump online at mystartjournal.com and let us know what you learned today.

YOU ARE NOT TOO YOUNG TO BE WISE
Now is the time

I am so proud of you! You are spending time every week reading the Word of the Lord, listening to what He is saying to you through the scripture and then telling someone what God has given to you.

You are becoming a very wise person. And you do not have to be my age (remember I do not tell my age) to be wise! But you do have to love wisdom more than foolishness. When I do or say something foolish I get upset at myself. When I do or say something that is wise I feel happy about myself. Now here's my dilemma, how can I be more wise than foolish?

The book of Proverbs is full of wisdom and is a great starting point. My friend, Annie, reads a chapter in Proverbs every day and she has done that since she was nine years old. No wonder she is a wise friend! Let's read some verses that got Annie on the "wise" road of her life. Let's work on it together today!

Scripture:

Proverbs 1:2-4,7

Proverbs teach you wisdom and train you. They help you understand wise sayings. They provide you with training and help you live wisely. They lead to what is right and honest and fair. They give understanding to childish people. They give knowledge and good sense to those who are young. If you really want to gain knowledge, you must begin by having respect for the Lord. But foolish people hate wisdom and training.

WEEK 5

S - Scripture (Read the scripture out loud slowly.)
Write the part of the scripture that stands out to you. It might be a phrase or a line or even just a word.

_____

T - Think (Read the scripture slowly again.)
Think about what the scripture is saying. How does this fit your life right now?

_____

_____

_____

_____

A - Ask (One more time...read the scripture slowly.)
Write a prayer about what God is showing you through the scripture.

_____

_____

_____

_____

R - Rest (Set your stopwatch for at least 2 - 5 minutes.)
Listen for God's still small voice (in your mind) saying who He is.
Finish this sentence, "God is my _____."

T - Tell
Tell an adult about what God has told you AND/OR you could jump online at mystartjournal.com and let us know what you learned today.

ANY YANKEE FANS OUT THERE?
Jesus gives me my identity

How about the Astros? L.A. Dodgers? How about the Cleveland Indians? You can usually tell a fan by the hat or shirt he wears. It's a sure giveaway!

When Jesus lived on the earth, there were beggars who were fake. They sat by the road side and pretended to be sick so that people would give them money. The governnment gave out coats to recognize those who truly were sick, so that people would identify them as genuine and help them.

A beggar named Bartimaeus was blind and he wore one of the government coats. One day a very interesting thing happened. Jesus called to him and he threw off his coat - the very thing that had become his identity.

As Bartimaeus cried out to Jesus, people told him to be quiet, but he cried out more saying "Have mercy on me!". Jesus stopped and called for him. Oh, I am excited to see what else you discover about Jesus and the blind man in today's Lectio Divina!

Scripture:
Mark 10:50-52
He threw his coat to one side. Then he jumped to his feet and came to Jesus. "What do you want me to do for you?" Jesus asked him. The blind man said, "Rabbi, I want to be able to see." "Go," said Jesus. "Your faith has healed you." Right away he could see. And he followed Jesus along the road.

S - Scripture (Read the scripture out loud slowly.)
Write the part of the scripture that stands out to you. It might be a phrase or a line or even just a word.

_____

T - Think (Read the scripture slowly again.)
Think about what the scripture is saying. How does this fit your life right now?

_____

_____

_____

_____

A - Ask (One more time...read the scripture slowly.)
Write a prayer about what God is showing you through the scripture.

_____

_____

_____

_____

R - Rest (Set your stopwatch for at least 2 - 5 minutes.)
Listen for God's still small voice (in your mind) saying who He is.
Finish this sentence, "God is my _____."

T - Tell
Tell an adult about what God has told you AND/OR you could jump online at mystartjournal.com and let us know what you learned today.

WHAT I WANT TO BE KNOWN FOR
Developing a good reputation

The book of Proverbs was written by a really wise man. Some say Solomon was the wisest man ever to live. It's full of simple sentences that are filled with truth. I remember as a kid memorizing today's verse, which talks about how even kids are known by the things they do.

Your favorite athlete is known for what he does for the team. Your favorite actor or singer is famous for the things they do. Kids are the same. What do you want to be known for?

Sometimes we do the wrong thing, and we start making a bad name for ourselves at school or in our neighborhoods. But it's not too late. You can turn it around by changing the things you do.

Show kindness. Look after those that others overlook. Be creative and find ways to be good to those around you. Soon enough, your reputation will chase after you. Your actions will speak louder than any words you speak.

Why don't you put this verse to memory! Get busy showing kindness today.

Scripture:
Proverbs 20:11
A child is known by his actions. He is known by whether his conduct is pure and right.

S - Scripture (Read the scripture out loud slowly.)
Write the part of the scripture that stands out to you. It might be a phrase or a line or even just a word.

_____

T - Think (Read the scripture slowly again.)
Think about what the scripture is saying. How does this fit your life right now?

_____

_____

_____

_____

A - Ask (One more time...read the scripture slowly.)
Write a prayer about what God is showing you through the scripture.

_____

_____

_____

_____

R - Rest (Set your stopwatch for at least 2 - 5 minutes.)
Listen for God's still small voice (in your mind) saying who He is.
Finish this sentence, "God is my _____."

T - Tell
Tell an adult about what God has told you AND/OR you could jump online at mystartjournal.com and let us know what you learned today.

GOD IS AN INVENTOR
I am God's invention

Thomas Edison created the light bulb and is called the Father of Electricity. From an early age he was inventing and creating things. He received the first of his 1,093 U.S. patents by age 22. Some people say, that by the age six, Thomas Edison's experiments with fire were responsible for burning down his father's barn! Soon after that, Edison tried to launch the first human balloon by getting a friend to swallow large quantities of fizzing powders to inflate himself with gas! Let's just say that the results were explosive. Thomas worked his creative genius to make things work.

Edison was an inventor, but God is a creator and His most amazing invention is YOU! You are His work. Think about this, whether you are working at school or doing your homework at home, God is working on You! You are like a piece of clay in the Potter's hands. He is molding, shaping and making you into what you were designed to be.

You are His Creation.

Scripture:
Ephesians 2:10
We are God's creation. He created us to belong to Christ Jesus. Now we can do good works. Long ago God had prepared these works for us to do.

S - Scripture (Read the scripture out loud slowly.)
Write the part of the scripture that stands out to you. It might be a phrase or a line or even just a word.

_____

T - Think (Read the scripture slowly again.)
Think about what the scripture is saying. How does this fit your life right now?

_____

_____

_____

_____

A - Ask (One more time...read the scripture slowly.)
Write a prayer about what God is showing you through the scripture.

_____

_____

_____

_____

R - Rest (Set your stopwatch for at least 2 - 5 minutes.)
Listen for God's still small voice (in your mind) saying who He is.
Finish this sentence, "God is my _____."

T - Tell
Tell an adult about what God has told you AND/OR you could jump online at mystartjournal.com and let us know what you learned today.

FRIENDS WHO REALLY CARE
My identity with good friends

One of my son's best friends, Alex, was hit by a car while riding his bike. He had to be rushed to the hospital to have surgery. After his surgery he had to use crutches. The good part is that he was fully healed in three months. The bad part was he had to miss the whole soccer season and he was one of his team's best players.

The team members talked about how they could be a good friend to Alex while he was recuperating, God's Word gave them some great ideas. I am excited to see what word or phrase God shows you as we read about how you can be a good friend in today's Lectio Divina.

Maybe you're not going to bring your friend to Jesus by cutting a hole in a roof, but think about what you can do for your friends to help them see the love of Jesus.

I have a big hunch you are going to be very creative about how you can care for a friend, too.

Scripture:
Mark 2:4-5a, 10b-11
But they could not get him close to Jesus because of the crowd. So they made a hole in the roof above Jesus. Then they lowered the man through it on a mat. Jesus saw their faith....Then Jesus spoke to the man who could not walk. "I tell you," he said, "Get up. Take your mat and go home."

S - Scripture (Read the scripture out loud slowly.)
Write the part of the scripture that stands out to you. It might be a phrase or a line or even just a word.

_____

T - Think (Read the scripture slowly again.)
Think about what the scripture is saying. How does this fit your life right now?

_____

_____

_____

_____

A - Ask (One more time...read the scripture slowly.)
Write a prayer about what God is showing you through the scripture.

_____

_____

_____

_____

R - Rest (Set your stopwatch for at least 2 - 5 minutes.)
Listen for God's still small voice (in your mind) saying who He is.
Finish this sentence, "God is my _____."

T - Tell
Tell an adult about what God has told you AND/OR you could jump online at mystartjournal.com and let us know what you learned today.

CAN ANYTHING GOOD COME FROM THERE?
Come and see

I love telling my friends about fun new things I have found, like... a new flavor of cookie, a new song on the radio or a new place to eat. Some of the people in my town are really fussy about their coffee. Some people would probably call them coffee snobs. If their coffee is too bitter, they won't drink it. If I said to them, "Hey, the local store is selling new coffee," I can imagine them asking me, "Can anything good come from there? The reputation of that place isn't really that great that it would produce something so good."

In today's Lectio Divina you will read the story of one of Jesus' followers inviting his friend to follow Jesus, and he asked the same question, "Can anything good come from Nazareth?" And Philip said, "Come and see for yourself."

Next time you wonder if something is good, don't take someone else's word for it. Go and have a look for yourself.

Scripture:
John 1:43-46
The next day Jesus decided to leave for Galilee. He found Philip and said to him, "Follow me." Philip was from the town of Bethsaida. So were Andrew and Peter. Philip found Nathanael and told him, "We have found the one whom Moses wrote about in the Law. The prophets also wrote about him. He is Jesus of Nazareth, the son of Joseph." "Nazareth! Can anything good come from there?" Nathanael asked. "Come and see," said Philip.

WEEK 10

S - Scripture (Read the scripture out loud slowly.)
Write the part of the scripture that stands out to you. It might be a phrase or a line or even just a word.

_____

T - Think (Read the scripture slowly again.)
Think about what the scripture is saying. How does this fit your life right now?

_____

_____

_____

_____

A - Ask (One more time...read the scripture slowly.)
Write a prayer about what God is showing you through the scripture.

_____

_____

_____

_____

R - Rest (Set your stopwatch for at least 2 - 5 minutes.)
Listen for God's still small voice (in your mind) saying who He is.
Finish this sentence, "God is my _____."

T - Tell
Tell an adult about what God has told you AND/OR you could jump online at mystartjournal.com and let us know what you learned today.

THE NIGHTSHIFT
God never sleeps

Several years ago I had to go into the ER late at night with one of my family members. We watched as the doctors and nurses went up and down the ward helping people. At about 10pm, the shift changed and all new doctors and nurses came to care for the patients. I remember thinking, "Wow, can you believe that they are going to work all night? I'd be way too tired." Some of you might know someone who works the nightshift. Well, did you know that GOD works the nightshift? He never sleeps. He is always watching us. Nothing goes on that He can't see. He does some of His best work when we can't see what He's doing.

He doesn't clock out. He doesn't tag team a new guy in. He's on the case 24/7. God is watching you and looking after you. You know why? Because God never sleeps, you can sleep in peace, without bad dreams, trusting that God is looking after you.

As we do today's Lectio Divina, the psalmist lifts his head to God and remembers a beautiful truth. God never sleeps. Think about that, whoa!

Scripture:
Psalm 121:3-4
He won't let your foot slip. He who watches over you won't get tired. In fact, he who watches over Israel won't get tired or go to sleep.

S - Scripture (Read the scripture out loud slowly.)
Write the part of the scripture that stands out to you. It might be a phrase or a line or even just a word.

_____

T - Think (Read the scripture slowly again.)
Think about what the scripture is saying. How does this fit your life right now?

_____

_____

_____

_____

A - Ask (One more time...read the scripture slowly.)
Write a prayer about what God is showing you through the scripture.

_____

_____

_____

_____

R - Rest (Set your stopwatch for at least 2 - 5 minutes.)
Listen for God's still small voice (in your mind) saying who He is.
Finish this sentence, "God is my _____."

T - Tell
Tell an adult about what God has told you AND/OR you could jump online at mystartjournal.com and let us know what you learned today.

I AM - JESUS
How you would describe Jesus

Let's pretend you are telling me a story about someone. The funny thing is, the more you describe them, the more I feel like I know them. Then you tell me who it is and I laugh and say, "Hey, she is my cousin!" You described her perfectly!

Jesus is really good at describing Himself as well. Oh, I am so interested in hearing which description you think shows Jesus' identity the best!

Scripture:
John 6:35, 48, 51
Then Jesus said, "I am the bread of life. Whoever comes to me will never go hungry. And whoever believes in me will never be thirsty. I am the bread of life. I am the living bread that came down from heaven. Everyone who eats some of this bread will live forever. This bread is my body. I will give it for the life of the world."

John 8:12; 9:5
Jesus spoke to the people again. He said, "I am the light of the world. Anyone who follows me will never walk in darkness. They will have that light. They will have life. While I am in the world, I am the light of the world."

John 10:7, 9
So Jesus said again, "What I'm about to tell you is true. I am like a gate for the sheep. Anyone who enters through me will be saved. They will come in and go out. And they will find plenty of food."

WEEK 12

S - Scripture (Read the scripture out loud slowly.)
Write the part of the scripture that stands out to you. It might be a phrase or a line or even just a word.

_____

T - Think (Read the scripture slowly again.)
Think about what the scripture is saying. How does this fit your life right now?

_____

_____

_____

_____

A - Ask (One more time...read the scripture slowly.)
Write a prayer about what God is showing you through the scripture.

_____

_____

_____

_____

R - Rest (Set your stopwatch for at least 2 - 5 minutes.)
Listen for God's still small voice (in your mind) saying who He is.
Finish this sentence, "God is my _____."

T - Tell
Tell an adult about what God has told you AND/OR you could jump online at mystartjournal.com and let us know what you learned today.

TIME FOR A HEART CHECK-UP

"God, see what is in my heart. Know what is there. Test me. Know what I'm thinking."
Psalm 139:23

Now is the time to reflect on your journey and do a HEART CHECK-UP.

Use the three questions below to guide three prayer conversations with God.

Dear God ...

1. During the last quarter, what did I learn about You and about myself?

2. What were You highlighting to me from this quarter on Identity?

3. What action steps would You like me to take?

1.

2.

3.

CHARACTER
MY ATTITUDE

Penny's Short Stories - CHARACTER

What was your favorite gift on your last birthday? One of my favorite gifts to receive is expensive perfume. If you buy cheap perfume, it often doesn't smell very nice or it doesn't last very long. Expensive perfume, has been tested and tried and is worth saving up for. In Bible days, perfume was considered to be very valuable. The other day, I was reading this verse in Ecclesiastes. Chapter 7 verse 1 says, "A good name is better than fine perfume."

A reputation is what is known about a person because of something they have done. Have you heard of Michael Jordan? He was a great basketball player in the 1990s. Everyone wanted to be number 23 when they played basketball, me included! He was on the winning championship team six times and is in the Basketball Hall of Fame. Because of his achievements, he has developed a reputation as a great basketballer. Do you know someone who has a good reputation? How about you? What are you known for?

As we look at Character this term, we will learn all about the kind of character God wants us to have and how we develop it. But before you start on the next Lectio, meet one of my students and hear her story.

Hey there,
I'm Alicia.
I live with my mom and Grandma in an apartment block in the city. I love going to school each day with my friends from our building. My friends know everything about me. We love hanging out together and having fun. We love slurpees, candy and talking about clothes and looking for the latest hairstyles online. Middle School isn't as bad as I thought it was going to be.

Last year in Miss Penny's class we talked about the kind of people we want to be and what we want to be remembered for. It reminded me of something that had happened to my friends and me.

Each day we get our lunch from the school cafeteria. The servers are known for being, well, let's just say it, grumpy. One day, a new worker started. She was so happy to be working. You could tell because she was always smiling. Fiona was a lovely lady and was always kind. She became known among the students as "Happy Fiona". By looking at her, you would think that she was the happiest person in the world. Miss Penny asked my friends and me to interview "Happy Fiona" for the school newspaper. So we arranged an interview. What we learned shocked us. She told us her story. She had grown up without any parents and spent her life in foster care. At the age of 15 she ran away and lied about her age. She worked in diners and restaurants as a waitress and got married pretty young. Her marriage was good and she was happy, but her husband was killed in a car accident when she was pregnant with their first child. When her baby arrived, she was so lonely and lost. She turned to her local church for help, and said "Yes!" to Jesus. She finally had the family she had dreamt of her whole life. Fiona could never dream of having so many people to love her. She hadn't felt joy like that before. She determined that everywhere she was, she would let the joy she felt show on her face.

My friends and I came away from that interview so challenged. Fiona wanted to be known as a person full of Joy, and she was. She had every reason to give up and surrender to her circumstances, but instead she chose Joy. Her everyday choice to smile at the future, not only affected her own son, but many others as she served in local school cafeterias.

My friends and I submitted our article to Miss Penny, and then we decided to do something special for Happy Fiona. We sold lollipops at school and used the money to buy her a lovely card and some flowers to say, "thanks for brightening our day with your smile". It was the first time I had ever seen her cry, haha.

I want to be known for the good things I do, just like Fiona.

Alicia

A good reputation is achieved by consistently behaving in a certain way, so that you become known by the things you do. And it's not just for adults. Proverbs 20:11 says that, "Even small children are known by their actions." Good or Bad. What you repeat, will be what you are known for. Okay, it's time to learn how to make sure we are representing Jesus well in ALL we do and say.

THE BIGGEST SANDCASTLE IN THE WORLD
Obedience

Okay friends, let's grab some shovels and buckets and head to the beach! I love to make sandcastles, but I hate watching the tide come in and destroy my creation. So sad!

The biggest sandcastle according to the Guinness Book of Records was built in India on February 10, 2017. It took 45 people to build a staggering 14.84 meters (48 foot 8 inches) tall castle with a base circumference of 161.54 meters (530 feet). Picture yourself being on the fifth floor of a hotel and looking down. That's how high it was! This gigantic castle was made entirely by hand (no big machines) and took nine days. Just for fun, you may want to google sandcastles and see more enormous ones!

As gigantic as this castle was, no one could ever live in it and that's the point of Jesus' words today. Anyone can build a house on the sand (a foolish builder) or on the rock (a wise builder). The choice is yours.

Obedience is pretty high on Jesus' list!

Scripture:
Matthew 7: 24-29

"So then, everyone who hears my words and puts them into practice is like a wise man. He builds his house on the rock. The rain comes down. The water rises. The winds blow and beat against that house. But it does not fall. It is built on the rock. But everyone who hears my words and does not put them into practice is like a foolish man. He builds his house on sand. The rain comes down. The water rises. The winds blow and beat against that house. And it falls with a loud crash." Jesus finished saying all these things. The crowds were amazed at his teaching. He taught like one who had authority. He did not speak like their teachers of the law.

S - Scripture (Read the scripture out loud slowly.)
Write the part of the scripture that stands out to you. It might be a phrase or a line or even just a word.

_____

T - Think (Read the scripture slowly again.)
Think about what the scripture is saying. How does this fit your life right now?

_____

_____

_____

_____

A - Ask (One more time...read the scripture slowly.)
Write a prayer about what God is showing you through the scripture.

_____

_____

_____

_____

R - Rest (Set your stopwatch for at least 2 - 5 minutes.)
Listen for God's still small voice (in your mind) saying who He is.
Finish this sentence, "God is my _____."

T - Tell
Tell an adult about what God has told you AND/OR you could jump online at mystartjournal.com and let us know what you learned today.

GROWING IN SECRET PLACES
Growth

Hey kids! Here's a large word for today's Lectio Divina... theology! Theology is the study of God and how His plans benefit the way you live your life. I love theology! Let's pay attention to what God is doing below the surface. He is always working, even in places you cannot see.

That reminds me of a Chinese Bamboo Seed my neighbor planted six years ago. When Jim planted the seed, he was faithful to water it and fertilize it. One year went by, nothing happened. He watered and fertilized it again in year two...nothing was seen. Year four and year five came and went, still nothing.

In the fifth year something extraordinary happened. The bamboo tree sprouted and grew up to 24.38 meters (80 feet). It was the tallest tree in the whole neighborhood and Jim was the gardening hero on Cutler Road! Through all these years the tree was growing underground and the root system grew strong first.

You have a 'root system' too. It's about being hidden in Christ. The Bible tells us we need to 'die' to our selfish desires and let Him work in the secret places in our lives.

Well, my Lectio friends, let's dive deep into some good theology today!

Scripture:
Colossians 2:6-7
You received Christ Jesus as Lord. So keep on living your lives in him. Have your roots in him. Build yourselves up in him. Grow strong in what you believe, just as you were taught. Be more thankful than ever before.

S - Scripture (Read the scripture out loud slowly.)
Write the part of the scripture that stands out to you. It might be a phrase or a line or even just a word.

_____

T - Think (Read the scripture slowly again.)
Think about what the scripture is saying. How does this fit your life right now?

_____

_____

_____

_____

A - Ask (One more time...read the scripture slowly.)
Write a prayer about what God is showing you through the scripture.

_____

_____

_____

_____

R - Rest (Set your stopwatch for at least 2 - 5 minutes.)
Listen for God's still small voice (in your mind) saying who He is.
Finish this sentence, "God is my _____."

T - Tell
Tell an adult about what God has told you AND/OR you could jump online at mystartjournal.com and let us know what you learned today.

HOW GOD PICKS A LEADER
Authenticity

It was near election time in my city and a friend of mine was running for office and he asked me to campaign for him. I told him he would be a great candidate and I would be happy to join his campaign. So, I wore a t-shirt with his name on it and handed out some great information about him to a lot of people. I thought for sure he would win but, sad to say, he lost.

God told the prophet Samuel to go to Bethlehem because it was election time and he would find a new king, but no one would vote, only God. Samuel was to go to Jesse's house because the new king would be one of Jesse's sons.

Samuel looked at seven of Jesse's sons and when he asked God to show him who the next king would be, God said, "I do not look at how someone appears on the outside, but I look at what is in the heart." You will now read in your Lectio Divina about how God found David.

What a story!

Scripture:

I Samuel 16: 11-13

So, he (Samuel) asked Jesse, "Are these the only sons you have?" "No," Jesse answered. "My younger son is taking care of the sheep." Samuel said, "Send for him. We won't sit down to eat until he arrives." So Jesse sent for his son and had him brought in. His skin was tanned. He had a fine appearance and handsome features. Then the Lord said, "Get up and anoint him. He is the one." So Samuel got the animal horn that was filled with olive oil. He anointed David in front of his brothers. From that day on, the Spirit of the Lord came on David with power. Samuel went back to Ramah.

S - Scripture (Read the scripture out loud slowly.)
Write the part of the scripture that stands out to you. It might be a phrase or a line or even just a word.

_____

T - Think (Read the scripture slowly again.)
Think about what the scripture is saying. How does this fit your life right now?

_____

_____

_____

_____

A - Ask (One more time...read the scripture slowly.)
Write a prayer about what God is showing you through the scripture.

_____

_____

_____

_____

R - Rest (Set your stopwatch for at least 2 - 5 minutes.)
Listen for God's still small voice (in your mind) saying who He is.
Finish this sentence, "God is my _____."

T - Tell
Tell an adult about what God has told you AND/OR you could jump online at mystartjournal.com and let us know what you learned today.

INTERESTED IN STARTING A BUSINESS?
Perseverance

When I was eight years old, I had a paper route business with my brother. The worst part of the business was the old man who yelled at us all the time. The best part was that we saved enough money to buy a puppy. That puppy's name was "Fancy Dancer" and she had three litters of puppies. That became my second business ... selling cute, adorable puppies!

Has God put an idea in you to start a business? Lydia was a business woman in the book of Acts. She was a "seller of purple". Purple fabric was very expensive and here's why. Lydia would find shellfish and when the veins in this fish were exposed to the sun, they turned a deep purple which became a dye for fabrics. Yes really, shellfish veins!

Paul, Silas, and Timothy came to the city of Philippi and walked outside the city gate to the river. They were looking for a place to pray and guess who they found?

Scripture:

Acts 16: 13-15

On the Sabbath day we went outside the city gate. We walked down to the river. There we expected to find a place of prayer. We sat down and began to speak to the women who had gathered together. One of those listening was a woman named Lydia. She was from the city of Thyatira. Her business was selling purple cloth. She was a worshiper of God. The Lord opened her heart to accept Paul's message. She and her family were baptized. Then she invited us to her home. "Do you consider me a believer in the Lord?" she asked. "If you do, come and stay at my house." She succeeded in getting us to go home with her.

S - Scripture (Read the scripture out loud slowly.)
Write the part of the scripture that stands out to you. It might be a phrase or a line or even just a word.

_____

T - Think (Read the scripture slowly again.)
Think about what the scripture is saying. How does this fit your life right now?

_____

_____

_____

_____

A - Ask (One more time...read the scripture slowly.)
Write a prayer about what God is showing you through the scripture.

_____

_____

_____

_____

R - Rest (Set your stopwatch for at least 2 - 5 minutes.)
Listen for God's still small voice (in your mind) saying who He is.
Finish this sentence, "God is my _____."

T - Tell
Tell an adult about what God has told you AND/OR you could jump online at mystartjournal.com and let us know what you learned today.

A GARDEN IN A PAPER CUP
Patience

When I was in third grade, my teacher gave us seeds to plant in soil that was in a Styrofoam cup. All I did was water it and put it on the window sill to get some sun and it grew! Amazing!

Jesus told make-believe stories that were called parables. One parable He told was about a farmer who threw seeds on the ground. Some fell on the hard path and the birds came and ate them. That's like people who have hard hearts.

Some seed fell near a pile of hard rocks and because the sun was hot and the seed did not have roots, they withered away and died. That's like people who have shallow character and when trouble comes, they run.

Some seeds fell on weeds and thorns. The thorns grew faster and taller than the seeds and took all the sunlight, so the seeds were choked out by the thorns. Those weeds and thorns are like worries and stress.

Now, Lectio Divina champions, let's read what Jesus said about the good soil. I would love to hear what He said to you out of this one amazing verse. I invite you to go online and tell me.

Scripture:
Mark 4:20
"And what is seed scattered on good soil like? The people hear the message. They accept it. They produce a good crop 30, 60, or even 100 times more than the farmer planted."

S - Scripture (Read the scripture out loud slowly.)
Write the part of the scripture that stands out to you. It might be a phrase or a line or even just a word.

_____

T - Think (Read the scripture slowly again.)
Think about what the scripture is saying. How does this fit your life right now?

_____

_____

_____

_____

A - Ask (One more time...read the scripture slowly.)
Write a prayer about what God is showing you through the scripture.

_____

_____

_____

_____

R - Rest (Set your stopwatch for at least 2 - 5 minutes.)
Listen for God's still small voice (in your mind) saying who He is.
Finish this sentence, "God is my _____."

T - Tell
Tell an adult about what God has told you AND/OR you could jump online at mystartjournal.com and let us know what you learned today.

WHAT A BAD DAY
Kindness

Mephibosheth was five years old. He hadn't done anything wrong. He was in a royal family and lived a privileged life, then all of a sudden, everything went downhill. His grandfather, Saul and his dad, Jonathan, died on the VERY same day. His family then had to escape the palace, and as the household fled in panic, Mephibosheth was hurt. From that day on, he could never walk again. Talk about a bad day!

However, this story has a happy ending. Several years later David became king. He remembered his promise to care for Jonathan's family. He asked his servant if there was anyone he could show God's kindness to. After reminding him about Mephibosheth, David then invited Jonathan's son to the palace to live and eat with him. Some of Mephibosheth's family had been mean to David earlier in his life, so it was amazing that he still decided to show kindness to Mephibosheth.

What a question for us to ask! Is there anyone that you could show God's kindness to today? God wants to show His kindness to people, but He needs your help.

Scripture:
2 Samuel 9:3-4
The king asked, "Isn't there anyone still alive from the royal house of Saul? God has been very kind to me. I would like to be kind to that person in the same way." Ziba answered the king, "A son of Jonathan is still living. Both of his feet were hurt so that he can't walk." "Where is he?" the king asked. Ziba answered, "He's in the town of Lo Debar. He's staying at the house of Makir, the son of Ammiel."

Mephibosheth ended up going to the palace and stayed with David. He ate at the King's table and was looked after by David the rest of his life.

WEEK 19

S - Scripture (Read the scripture out loud slowly.)
Write the part of the scripture that stands out to you. It might be a phrase or a line or even just a word.

_____

T - Think (Read the scripture slowly again.)
Think about what the scripture is saying. How does this fit your life right now?

_____

_____

_____

_____

A - Ask (One more time...read the scripture slowly.)
Write a prayer about what God is showing you through the scripture.

_____

_____

_____

_____

R - Rest (Set your stopwatch for at least 2 - 5 minutes.)
Listen for God's still small voice (in your mind) saying who He is.
Finish this sentence, "God is my _____."

T - Tell
Tell an adult about what God has told you AND/OR you could jump online at mystartjournal.com and let us know what you learned today.

IT WORKS EVERY TIME
Faithfulness

Any place you live in the world, this demonstration will work... unless you live on the moon! Take two stones, one small and one big, hold them at the same height and drop them at the same time to the ground. Which one gets to the ground first? You are right, the big one and that's because of gravity. It works every time.

There are many things you can depend on. For example: summer, autumn, winter, and spring. Whoever heard of winter coming after spring? The stars are arranged in the same patterns every night, the moon has the same phases every month. These are all signs of God's dependability and faithfulness. And it works every time, too! That's just the way He is. Because He is faithful, He also gives you the ability to be faithful, too.

Let's do our Lectio Divina a little differently today. You will have references from three different books in the Bible. Remember to read them out loud slowly and see which word or phrase stands out to you. Ready? Go!

Scripture:
Psalm 100:5
The Lord is good. His faithful love continues forever.

Lamentations 3:22-23
The Lord loves us very much. So we haven't been completely destroyed. His loving concern never fails. His great love is new every morning. Lord, how faithful you are!

Hebrews 10:23
Let us hold firmly to the hope we claim to have. The One who promised is faithful.

S - Scripture (Read the scripture out loud slowly.)
Write the part of the scripture that stands out to you. It might be a phrase or a line or even just a word.

_____

T - Think (Read the scripture slowly again.)
Think about what the scripture is saying. How does this fit your life right now?

_____

_____

_____

_____

A - Ask (One more time...read the scripture slowly.)
Write a prayer about what God is showing you through the scripture.

_____

_____

_____

_____

R - Rest (Set your stopwatch for at least 2 - 5 minutes.)
Listen for God's still small voice (in your mind) saying who He is.
Finish this sentence, "God is my _____."

T - Tell
Tell an adult about what God has told you AND/OR you could jump online at mystartjournal.com and let us know what you learned today.

HOW DO I LOVE YOU?
Compassion

This really happened to my cousin, Joyce, when she was in fifth grade. A lady came to her church and everything she had was in a garbage bag. She had no place to go and my cousin pleaded with my aunt to bring the lady home to their house so they could feed her and she could sleep in a warm bed. My aunt, uncle, and my two cousins decided they would bring the lady home with them. She stayed for one week and was very mean to my aunt. I heard stories of how she yelled at her and demanded my aunt serve her.

When that week was over, their church provided for the lady to stay in a hotel, took meals to her and befriended her. Christmas rolled around a few weeks later and the lady came to my cousins' house bringing everyone Christmas presents. She told them how much she loved them. She said she knew God was in their home because of the love and compassion they all showed to her, especially my aunt. That lady knew Jesus was real!

Your Lectio Divina today is about Jesus, who showed more compassion than anyone else ever has!

Scripture:
Matthew 20:29-34
Jesus and his disciples were leaving Jericho. A large crowd followed him. Two blind men were sitting by the side of the road. They heard that Jesus was going by. So they shouted, "Lord! Son of David! Have mercy on us!" The crowd commanded them to stop. They told them to be quiet. But the two men shouted even louder, "Lord! Son of David! Have mercy on us!" Jesus stopped and called out to them. "What do you want me to do for you?" he asked. "Lord," they answered, "we want to be able to see." Jesus felt deep concern for them. He touched their eyes. Right away they could see. And they followed him.

S - Scripture (Read the scripture out loud slowly.)
Write the part of the scripture that stands out to you. It might be a phrase or a line or even just a word.

_____

T - Think (Read the scripture slowly again.)
Think about what the scripture is saying. How does this fit your life right now?

_____

_____

_____

_____

A - Ask (One more time...read the scripture slowly.)
Write a prayer about what God is showing you through the scripture.

_____

_____

_____

_____

R - Rest (Set your stopwatch for at least 2 - 5 minutes.)
Listen for God's still small voice (in your mind) saying who He is.
Finish this sentence, "God is my _____."

T - Tell
Tell an adult about what God has told you AND/OR you could jump online at mystartjournal.com and let us know what you learned today.

JESUS WAS BULLIED
Assertiveness

Did you know that more than 160,000 school children stay home from school every day because they are afraid of being bullied? These kids (and you may be one of them) feel small and hate themselves. For many, the problem does not "go away."

Jesus was bullied when he was slapped on the face by the guard of the High Priest. He did not turn His face so the guard could slap him again. Instead Jesus replied, "Have I said something wrong?. If I have, give witness to it. But if I spoke the truth, why did you hit me?" He confronted the bully and demanded an answer for His unjust treatment. Jesus was not mean, but He was assertive.

Did you know that Joseph, Moses, David, Shadrach, Meshach, Abednego and many others in the Bible were all bullied? God does not approve of anyone bullying any child or adult.

My dear Lectio Divina friends, I am praying today for your protection. If you see someone being bullied, God is probably asking you to pray for him or her and to be a friend who is loyal to them.

It is especially important to read this scripture and to read it with confidence in a loud, slow voice, declaring God's heart of protection and care for you.

Scripture:
Psalm 91:14-16
The Lord says, "I will save the one who loves me. I will keep him safe, because he trusts in me. He will call out to me, and I will answer him. I will be with him in times of trouble. I will save him and honor him. I will give him a long and full life. I will save him."

WEEK 22

S - Scripture (Read the scripture out loud slowly.)
Write the part of the scripture that stands out to you. It might be a phrase or a line or even just a word.

_____

T - Think (Read the scripture slowly again.)
Think about what the scripture is saying. How does this fit your life right now?

_____

_____

_____

_____

A - Ask (One more time...read the scripture slowly.)
Write a prayer about what God is showing you through the scripture.

_____

_____

_____

_____

R - Rest (Set your stopwatch for at least 2 - 5 minutes.)
Listen for God's still small voice (in your mind) saying who He is.
Finish this sentence, "God is my _____ ."

T - Tell
Tell an adult about what God has told you AND/OR you could jump online at mystartjournal.com and let us know what you learned today.

I AM...?
Confidence

OK, my Lectio friends, let's play a game! In the spaces below, write two sentences that describe you.

I am _____.

I am _____.

I wish I could read your answers! I'll bet some of them are serious and some are funny! The best part though, is that your answers are about YOU! Hey, better yet, go online and tell me and your friends around the world what you wrote!

Knowing who I am builds confidence and confidence makes me strong on the inside. If I am strong on the inside I am most likely, strong on the outside.

Now, let's say out loud the following "I am's":

I am God's child! (John 1:12)

I am a friend of Jesus! (John 15:15)

I am chosen by God! (Ephesians 1:4)

I am a citizen of heaven! (Philippians 3:20)

I am chosen and appointed to bear fruit! (John 15:16)

I am confident I can do all things through Christ who strengthens me! (Philippians 4:13)

Over 3,000 years ago, David wrote Psalm 139. We are choosing verses 13-14 and believe as you participate in the Lectio Divina, God will give you more and more confidence in how wonderful it is to be His kid. I really want to see what word or phrase God is making real to you.

Scripture:
Psalm 139:13-14
You created the deepest parts of my being. You put me together inside my mother's body. How you made me is amazing and wonderful. I praise you for that. What you have done is wonderful. I know that very well.

WEEK 23

S - Scripture (Read the scripture out loud slowly.)
Write the part of the scripture that stands out to you. It might be a phrase
or a line or even just a word.

_____

T - Think (Read the scripture slowly again.)
Think about what the scripture is saying. How does this fit your life right now?

_____

_____

_____

_____

A - Ask (One more time...read the scripture slowly.)
Write a prayer about what God is showing you through the scripture.

_____

_____

_____

_____

R - Rest (Set your stopwatch for at least 2 - 5 minutes.)
Listen for God's still small voice (in your mind) saying who He is.
Finish this sentence, "God is my _____."

T - Tell
Tell an adult about what God has told you AND/OR you could jump online at
mystartjournal.com and let us know what you learned today.

JESUS THE CHEF
Thoughtfulness

You know what would be so fun? Building a fire on the beach and roasting hot dogs together along with some yummy s'mores. Jesus did that once. Well, not with hot dogs and s'mores, but with bread and grilled fish for His friends.

After Jesus' resurrection, the disciples were discouraged not having Jesus around and they returned to fishing. After a long and exhausting night, they caught nothing. They didn't know Jesus was watching them as their boat came near shore. He called to them and asked if they had any fish. Of course the discouraged disciples said, "No". He then told them to throw out the net on the right side of the boat and BOOM … 153 fish filled that net! They knew it had to be Jesus talking with them.

When they got to the shore with their catch, Jesus had already made breakfast for them. He knew they would be exhausted. He knew they were questioning what was ahead for them without Him being there. He knew they were discouraged. Rather than scolding them for going back to their old life, he blessed them with the most thoughtful gift - 153 fish along with breakfast for his tired friends! How thoughtful is that?

Scripture:
John 21:12-14
Jesus said to them, "Come and have breakfast." None of the disciples dared to ask him, "Who are you?" They knew it was the Lord. Jesus came, took the bread and gave it to them. He did the same thing with the fish. This was the third time Jesus appeared to his disciples after he was raised from the dead.

WEEK 24

S - Scripture (Read the scripture out loud slowly.)
Write the part of the scripture that stands out to you. It might be a phrase or a line or even just a word.

_____

T - Think (Read the scripture slowly again.)
Think about what the scripture is saying. How does this fit your life right now?

_____

_____

_____

_____

A - Ask (One more time...read the scripture slowly.)
Write a prayer about what God is showing you through the scripture.

_____

_____

_____

_____

R - Rest (Set your stopwatch for at least 2 - 5 minutes.)
Listen for God's still small voice (in your mind) saying who He is.
Finish this sentence, "God is my _____."

T - Tell
Tell an adult about what God has told you AND/OR you could jump online at mystartjournal.com and let us know what you learned today.

STARTING VS. FINISHING &
FINISHING VS. WINNING
Commitment

There is a big difference between starting and finishing and a really big difference between finishing and winning! In the Summer Olympics of 2016, in Brazil, two female runners, Abbey from the U.S.A. and Nikki of New Zealand, were competing in the 5,000 meter event.

After about 3,200 meters, the two collided and fell to the ground. Abbey got up but saw that Nikki was hurt and stopped to help her. When Nikki felt Abbey's hand on her shoulder, all she heard her say was, "Get up, get up, we have to finish this!"

Finishing is a big deal. Personally, I believe finishers are winners, don't you? I'm very excited about you reading these two verses about running the race and how you can not only be a finisher, but help someone else finish well like Abbey did.

Scripture:
Hebrews 12:1-2
A huge cloud of witnesses is all around us. So let us throw off everything that stands in our way. Let us throw off any sin that holds on to us so tightly. Let us keep on running the race marked out for us. Let us keep looking to Jesus. He is the author of faith. He also makes it perfect. He paid no attention to the shame of the cross. He suffered there because of the joy he was looking forward to. Then he sat down at the right hand of the throne of God.

WEEK 25

S - Scripture (Read the scripture out loud slowly.)
Write the part of the scripture that stands out to you. It might be a phrase or a line or even just a word.

_____

T - Think (Read the scripture slowly again.)
Think about what the scripture is saying. How does this fit your life right now?

_____

_____

_____

_____

A - Ask (One more time...read the scripture slowly.)
Write a prayer about what God is showing you through the scripture.

_____

_____

_____

_____

R - Rest (Set your stopwatch for at least 2 - 5 minutes.)
Listen for God's still small voice (in your mind) saying who He is.
Finish this sentence, "God is my _____."

T - Tell
Tell an adult about what God has told you AND/OR you could jump online at mystartjournal.com and let us know what you learned today.

TIME FOR A HEART CHECK-UP

"God, see what is in my heart. Know what is there. Test me. Know what I'm thinking."
Psalm 139:23

Now is the time to reflect on your journey and do a HEART CHECK-UP.

Use the three questions below to guide three prayer conversations with God.

Dear God ...

1. During the last quarter, what did I learn about You and about myself?

2. What were You highlighting to me from this quarter on Identity?

3. What action steps would You like me to take?

WEEK 26

1.

2.

3.

ADVENTURE

MY JOURNEY

Penny's Short Stories- ADVENTURE

I love a good Choose Your Own Adventure Story. Some of my favorite stories to read with my classes are the stories where the students get to choose how the story ends. When God invited us into relationship with Him, through His son Jesus, He was inviting us into the most exciting story ever!

As we look at Adventure this quarter, we will learn all about the big life God wants us to live. We follow our Captain, Jesus to the very end. But before that, I want you to meet one of my students and here is his story.

Hey there,

I'm Phillip.

I'm in Grade 6 and just got back from a family vacation on a cruise ship. I loved watching the dolphins show off as they jumped in and out of the ocean. When we got home, I had to give a report to Miss Penny about something on my trip that I wasn't expecting and I told her about one of the nights in the Kids Club. On the cruise, my brother and I went to the Kids Club each night and on the second night they invited the Captain to come and give us a "Choose Your Own Adventure Talk." I'd never heard one of those before, but he was giving out free ice cream at the end of his story, so I stayed to listen.

His story really got me thinking. His story went like this.

Imagine this. You decide to sail across the ocean, but halfway across the ocean you get into some trouble along the way. The engine fails on your boat and you are left floating in the middle of the ocean. In the distance, you spot a cruise ship.

You can see the captain in the window. You know he has the power to save you. You know he can get you out of trouble. As commander and captain of the ship you want to be rescued. The captain rescues you. You love that you are safe, that you are saved, that you are no longer drowning. But then He invites you to follow Him.

He invites you to change direction and join his crew.

Partner in the adventure.

You have a big choice to make. Will you:

1. Let the Captain run your ship and all the future voyages. You say - YES to the Captain.

OR

2. You want to run your own ship. Even if you haven't been doing a great job. You say, NO to the Captain

OR

3. You want to be rescued, but you don't want the Captain to run every voyage of your life. So you say NO, to the Captain.

Once the story finished, he told us that God is like the Captain of this ship. He wants to help us and navigate our ship, but sometimes we think we know the best way to go. When we choose the adventure God has for us, then Captain Jesus will never leave us. His story made me think. I had made some choices last summer that weren't really that great, and had asked God to help me. He had helped me alright, but I had forgot all about it, and went back to doing things my way. The most unexpected thing that happened on my vacation, was being reminded that Jesus wants to Captain my ship. He has the BEST ADVENTURE planned, but I need to join His crew.

Phillip

God has the greatest adventure planned for you. If you're anything like me, I can sometimes forget that Jesus is my Captain and try to take the wheel myself. It usually doesn't end very well! As we learn about saying the big YES to God's best life for us, let's remember to say YES in the little things as well.

ARE WE THERE YET?
Learning to be patient

A friend of mine has a three year old, and they were headed on vacation to the beach. Even before they had even pulled out of the driveway, the little girl said, "Are we there yet?" Her parents laughed and told her, "No." But she didn't understand. She wanted to be at the beach, NOW. But they had to keep travelling to get there.

Have you ever been so eager to reach the destination that you got impatient? I know I have.

Our Christian walk is a journey. Let's have some fun. God has a great adventure planned for us if we will keep our eyes open for what He wants to show us. Stay on God's path, don't get sidetracked because things take longer than you thought. God has planned this adventure for you. For you to enjoy and give you hope for your life.

Enjoy the journey!

Obedience is pretty high on Jesus' list!

Scripture:

Jeremiah 29:11

"I know the plans I have for you," announces the Lord. "I want you to enjoy success. I do not plan to harm you. I will give you hope for the years to come."

WEEK 27

S - Scripture (Read the scripture out loud slowly.)
Write the part of the scripture that stands out to you. It might be a phrase or a line or even just a word.

_____

T - Think (Read the scripture slowly again.)
Think about what the scripture is saying. How does this fit your life right now?

_____

_____

_____

_____

A - Ask (One more time...read the scripture slowly.)
Write a prayer about what God is showing you through the scripture.

_____

_____

_____

_____

R - Rest (Set your stopwatch for at least 2 - 5 minutes.)
Listen for God's still small voice (in your mind) saying who He is.
Finish this sentence, "God is my _____."

T - Tell
Tell an adult about what God has told you AND/OR you could jump online at mystartjournal.com and let us know what you learned today.

LOST AT THE MALL
Getting Back On Track

I remember as a young child going shopping one evening with my family. My parents were looking at something in the store and I wandered away to look at something else. When I looked around, I couldn't find my parents anywhere. I searched the store for a long time, and couldn't find them. It seemed like I'd been round and round the same parts of the store for ages and I had no idea where I was going.

Sometimes when we wander, we get off track and find ourselves lost in the middle of nowhere. We walk around the same place over and over. Finally, I went to the front of the store and had the attendant call out over the loud speaker for my parents and they came and got me.

God will come running when you call His name too. Just so you know this is true, Jesus told a story about a lost son. There was a man who had two sons. The younger son asked his Father for a share of his inheritance and decided to pack up and leave home. Then he left the country and wasted all his money living a wild life. He spent all he had and was so hungry that he was willing to eat with the pigs. Somewhere in his adventure, he realized that he was much better off in his father's house. He decided to head home and take his chances and see what his father would do.

Can you guess what the father does? Check out their story in today's Lectio Divina.

Scripture:
Luke 15:20-24
"So he got up and went to his father. While the son was still a long way off, his father saw him. He was filled with tender love for his son. He ran to him. He threw his arms around him and kissed him. The son said to him, 'Father, I have sinned against heaven and against you. I am no longer fit to be called your son.' But the father said to his servants, 'Quick! Bring the best robe and put it on him. Put a ring on his finger and sandals on his feet. Bring the fattest calf and kill it. Let's have a feast and celebrate. This son of mine was dead. And now he is alive again. He was lost and now he is found.' So they began to celebrate."

S - Scripture (Read the scripture out loud slowly.)
Write the part of the scripture that stands out to you. It might be a phrase or a line or even just a word.

_____

T - Think (Read the scripture slowly again.)
Think about what the scripture is saying. How does this fit your life right now?

_____

_____

_____

_____

A - Ask (One more time…read the scripture slowly.)
Write a prayer about what God is showing you through the scripture.

_____

_____

_____

_____

R - Rest (Set your stopwatch for at least 2 - 5 minutes.)
Listen for God's still small voice (in your mind) saying who He is.
Finish this sentence, "God is my _____."

T - Tell
Tell an adult about what God has told you AND/OR you could jump online at mystartjournal.com and let us know what you learned today.

I'M NOT TOO SURE ABOUT THIS
The adventure of not knowing the future

I used to play basketball in high school. We had a really good team. Our best player was very tall and our strategy was pretty simple: pass the ball to Chantel and she'll get it in every time. Toward the end of the season, Chantel got sick and wasn't able to play. We turned up to play anyway and took one look at the team we were playing against and knew we had no chance. They were taller, they had cool basketball shoes and looked like really good players. We had lost the game in our minds before we even got on the court.

I wish I could tell you we beat the odds and won the game. We didn't and it was miserable. Thinking about it now, the story reminds me of a story in the Bible when the people of Israel were walking through the desert to their new home in Canaan. They sent some spies to check out the new land, and they freaked out at the people that lived there. You can read the whole story in Numbers 13.

What would have happened if they believed God's report instead of the bad report?

Scripture:
Numbers 13:31-33
But the men who had gone up with him said, "We are not able to go up against the people, for they are stronger than we." And they gave the children of Israel a bad report of the land which they had spied out, saying, "The land through which we have gone as spies is a land that devours its inhabitants, and all the people whom we saw in it are men of great stature. There we saw the giants; and we were like grasshoppers in our own sight, and so we were in their sight."

S - Scripture (Read the scripture out loud slowly.)
Write the part of the scripture that stands out to you. It might be a phrase or a line or even just a word.

_____

T - Think (Read the scripture slowly again.)
Think about what the scripture is saying. How does this fit your life right now?

_____

_____

_____

_____

A - Ask (One more time...read the scripture slowly.)
Write a prayer about what God is showing you through the scripture.

_____

_____

_____

_____

R - Rest (Set your stopwatch for at least 2 - 5 minutes.)
Listen for God's still small voice (in your mind) saying who He is.
Finish this sentence, "God is my _____."

T - Tell
Tell an adult about what God has told you AND/OR you could jump online at mystartjournal.com and let us know what you learned today.

THIS IS HOT
When the heat is on, you're not alone

Shadrach, Meshach and Abednego are known in history as the three Hebrew boys who got thrown into a big oven furnace by an evil King. Can you imagine being thrown into an oven like a pizza? No way!

The boys wouldn't bow to King Nebuchadnezzar. Instead, they trusted that God would protect them and be with them. When the men were thrown into the fire, the King was so angry, he turned the heat up even hotter.

But something amazing happened. They were not alone. As you do today's Lectio Divina, read what happened when the King looked into the furnace. What can we learn from this story?

Scripture:
Daniel 3:25-26
The king said, "Look! I see four men walking around in the fire. They aren't tied up. And the fire hasn't even harmed them. The fourth man looks like a son of the gods." Then the king approached the opening of the blazing furnace. He shouted, "Shadrach, Meshach and Abednego, come out! You who serve the Most High God, come here!" So they came out of the fire.

S - Scripture (Read the scripture out loud slowly.)
Write the part of the scripture that stands out to you. It might be a phrase or a line or even just a word.

_____

T - Think (Read the scripture slowly again.)
Think about what the scripture is saying. How does this fit your life right now?

_____

_____

_____

_____

A - Ask (One more time...read the scripture slowly.)
Write a prayer about what God is showing you through the scripture.

_____

_____

_____

_____

R - Rest (Set your stopwatch for at least 2 - 5 minutes.)
Listen for God's still small voice (in your mind) saying who He is.
Finish this sentence, "God is my _____."

T - Tell
Tell an adult about what God has told you AND/OR you could jump online at mystartjournal.com and let us know what you learned today.

GETTING ALONG WITH OTHERS
How God turns something bad to good

Getting along with others isn't always easy, and sometimes people who love each other can hurt one another with the words they say and things they do. Joseph's dad loved him and bought him a colorful coat. His brothers got really jealous. They put him in a ditch and sold him off to gypsies. Now that's taking sibling rivalry to the next level!

The story didn't get better right away for Joseph. He was mistreated, put in jail and forgotten about. But all through his life, God was with him and that made all the difference. Joseph realized that even though his family was mean to him, God actually had a plan. Joseph ended up helping his family through one of the worst famines of his time.

Joseph's family thought he was dead, and got the shock of their lives when they realized he was alive. Joseph could have been angry, but he wasn't.

Today, be inspired by how Joseph responded to his family when he finally saw them again after so many years.

Scripture:

Genesis 50:18-20

Then his brothers came and threw themselves down in front of him. "We are your slaves," they said. But Joseph said to them, "Don't be afraid. Do you think I'm God? You planned to harm me. But God planned it for good. He planned to do what is now being done. He wanted to save many lives."

S - Scripture (Read the scripture out loud slowly.)
Write the part of the scripture that stands out to you. It might be a phrase or a line or even just a word.

_____

T - Think (Read the scripture slowly again.)
Think about what the scripture is saying. How does this fit your life right now?

_____

_____

_____

_____

A - Ask (One more time...read the scripture slowly.)
Write a prayer about what God is showing you through the scripture.

_____

_____

_____

_____

R - Rest (Set your stopwatch for at least 2 - 5 minutes.)
Listen for God's still small voice (in your mind) saying who He is.
Finish this sentence, "God is my _____."

T - Tell
Tell an adult about what God has told you AND/OR you could jump online at mystartjournal.com and let us know what you learned today.

I MESSED UP
What happened to Peter when the pressure was on?

I don't like making mistakes and I really don't like disappointing people. When I was little I had a friend who would hide whenever she got upset and made a mistake. Her parents would find her and talk to her. She felt embarrassed and miserable, but in the end, hiding didn't help.

Have you ever gotten so upset that you wanted to hide away? Jesus had a friend who did that. His name was Peter. He said that he didn't know who Jesus was three times. He was embarrassed because he had let Jesus down.

If you have done this, then you are not alone. Today's Lectio Divina is a little sad. We've all been guilty for doing things that are wrong. Check out the story below and what Jesus did after Peter denied Him.

Scripture:
Luke 22:59-62
About an hour later, another person spoke up. "This fellow must have been with Jesus," he said. "He is from Galilee." Peter replied, "Man, I don't know what you're talking about!" Just as he was speaking, the rooster crowed. The Lord turned and looked right at Peter. Then Peter remembered what the Lord had spoken to him. "The rooster will crow today," Jesus had said. "Before it does, you will say three times that you don't know me." Peter went outside. He broke down and cried.

S - Scripture (Read the scripture out loud slowly.)
Write the part of the scripture that stands out to you. It might be a phrase or a line or even just a word.

_____

T - Think (Read the scripture slowly again.)
Think about what the scripture is saying. How does this fit your life right now?

_____

_____

_____

_____

A - Ask (One more time...read the scripture slowly.)
Write a prayer about what God is showing you through the scripture.

_____

_____

_____

_____

R - Rest (Set your stopwatch for at least 2 - 5 minutes.)
Listen for God's still small voice (in your mind) saying who He is.
Finish this sentence, "God is my _____."

T - Tell
Tell an adult about what God has told you AND/OR you could jump online at mystartjournal.com and let us know what you learned today.

NEED A GUIDE?
The Lord is my Shepherd

It's really hard when you don't know where you are going. Late one evening I was coming home from church and it was raining so hard, that I could barely see. My windshield wipers were working overtime but it didn't feel like they were helping. The sound of the rain on the roof of the car was so loud I couldn't hear the music playing. It was a little scary. All I could see were the blurry lights of the car in front of me. I followed that car until I found cover from the storm.

If it wasn't for the lights in front of me, guiding my way, I would have been in big trouble.

Shepherds in Israel look after their sheep through the seasons of the year. They care for their every need, walking them through dangerous valleys and protecting them from lions and bears. King David was a Shepherd. He wrote Psalm 23. When you read today's Lectio Divina, you'll see that he used his life experiences to think about who God is and how God looks after us.

Scripture:

Psalm 23:1-3

The Lord is my shepherd. He gives me everything I need. He lets me lie down in fields of green grass. He leads me beside quiet waters. He gives me new strength. He guides me in the right paths for the honor of his name.

S - Scripture (Read the scripture out loud slowly.)
Write the part of the scripture that stands out to you. It might be a phrase or a line or even just a word.

_____

T - Think (Read the scripture slowly again.)
Think about what the scripture is saying. How does this fit your life right now?

_____

_____

_____

_____

A - Ask (One more time...read the scripture slowly.)
Write a prayer about what God is showing you through the scripture.

_____

_____

_____

_____

R - Rest (Set your stopwatch for at least 2 - 5 minutes.)
Listen for God's still small voice (in your mind) saying who He is.
Finish this sentence, "God is my _____."

T - Tell
Tell an adult about what God has told you AND/OR you could jump online at mystartjournal.com and let us know what you learned today.

GET DIRECTIONS
The Bible helps us go the right way

One of my closest friends and I were traveling to a class on the other side of the city. I wasn't really sure of where I was going, but I didn't want to use a map. I know, I was being REALLY stubborn. I thought I knew best. I just wanted to pretend I knew my way, and see if we made it to the right place. Well, we didn't! We ended up way off course. I soon realized that if I had just checked the map, I would have known where to go.

Sometimes you have to stop, turn on the light, and check the map to go the right way.

God's words are found in the Bible and they light up our path. It gives us God's directions and helps prevent us from taking detours.

As you Lectio Divina today, ask God to help you use the map of His word to guide your heart.

Scripture:
Psalm 119:105
Your word is like a lamp that shows me the way. It is like a light that guides me.

S - Scripture (Read the scripture out loud slowly.)
Write the part of the scripture that stands out to you. It might be a phrase or a line or even just a word.

_____

T - Think (Read the scripture slowly again.)
Think about what the scripture is saying. How does this fit your life right now?

_____

_____

_____

_____

A - Ask (One more time...read the scripture slowly.)
Write a prayer about what God is showing you through the scripture.

_____

_____

_____

_____

R - Rest (Set your stopwatch for at least 2 - 5 minutes.)
Listen for God's still small voice (in your mind) saying who He is.
Finish this sentence, "God is my _____."

T - Tell
Tell an adult about what God has told you AND/OR you could jump online at mystartjournal.com and let us know what you learned today.

BUSY AS A BEE!
Deborah, a courageous leader

Did you know that 1,100 bees would have to visit four million flowers to make 1 kilogram (2.2 pounds) of honey? That's a lot of busy bees! Bees are the only insects that make food that people can eat. Bee hives are also called colonies and have one queen bee who lays up to 2,000 eggs a day. Hives can have up to 40,000 bees living in them!

I have a bee hive and we have an organic blueberry farm across the road from my house. My bees visit the blueberries and we have blueberry blossom honey! Mmm!

Deborah is a name that means "busy bee"! She lived 1,400 years before Jesus and was a prophetess, judge, and a great leader. Deborah told Barak, a general in the Israeli army, that God was going to give the army a big victory over their enemy and He would go ahead of them. That was a prophecy God gave to her.

How did this happen? Deborah and Barak sang a song of praise together to the Lord after the BIG victory. God sent a flood and the chariots of the enemy's army got stuck in the mud. That's how the Israeli army won! Wow! All because God sent His word to Deborah and she gave it to Barak! I can't wait to hear what God is saying to you today.

Scripture:

Judges 4:15-16

As Barak's men marched out the Lord drove Sisera (the leader of the enemy army) away from the field of battle. He scattered all of Sisera's chariots. Barak's men struck down Sisera's army with their swords. Sisera left his chariot behind. He ran away on foot. But Barak chased Sisera's chariots and army. He chased them all the way to Harosheth Haggoyim. All of Sisera's men were killed with swords. Not even one was left.

S - Scripture (Read the scripture out loud slowly.)
Write the part of the scripture that stands out to you. It might be a phrase or a line or even just a word.

_____

T - Think (Read the scripture slowly again.)
Think about what the scripture is saying. How does this fit your life right now?

_____

_____

_____

_____

A - Ask (One more time...read the scripture slowly.)
Write a prayer about what God is showing you through the scripture.

_____

_____

_____

_____

R - Rest (Set your stopwatch for at least 2 - 5 minutes.)
Listen for God's still small voice (in your mind) saying who He is.
Finish this sentence, "God is my _____."

T - Tell
Tell an adult about what God has told you AND/OR you could jump online at mystartjournal.com and let us know what you learned today.

A FOSTER CHILD BECOMES A QUEEN
The story of Esther's courage

Today's Lectio Divina really shows us how much God loves children. Some of your friends, and perhaps, you too, have experienced some very sad times in your life.

Esther's parents died when she was a little girl. Her Uncle Mordecai took care of her and became her guardian, so that made her a foster child. When Esther grew up she entered a beauty contest to see who would be the next queen of Persia. And she won!

Esther's Uncle Mordecai was so proud of her. He missed her when she moved into the palace. There was a mean man named Haman who tricked King Xerxes into killing all the Jews. Mordecai knew that Esther could save their lives if she would tell the King, but she was afraid the King would be angry with her.

This is what Uncle Mordecai told Esther:

Scripture:
Esther 4:13
He said, "You live in the king's palace. But don't think that just because you are there you will be the only Jew who will escape. What if you don't say anything at this time? Then help for the Jews will come from another place. But you and your family will die. Who knows? It's possible that you became queen for a time just like this."

Esther listened to her uncle and she asked her husband, the King, to save the lives of all the Jews. And he did. Esther was brave. All her family was saved.

S - Scripture (Read the scripture out loud slowly.)
Write the part of the scripture that stands out to you. It might be a phrase or a line or even just a word.

_____

T - Think (Read the scripture slowly again.)
Think about what the scripture is saying. How does this fit your life right now?

_____

_____

_____

_____

A - Ask (One more time...read the scripture slowly.)
Write a prayer about what God is showing you through the scripture.

_____

_____

_____

_____

R - Rest (Set your stopwatch for at least 2 - 5 minutes.)
Listen for God's still small voice (in your mind) saying who He is.
Finish this sentence, "God is my _____."

T - Tell
Tell an adult about what God has told you AND/OR you could jump online at mystartjournal.com and let us know what you learned today.

THE BIGGEST VOLUNTEER IN HISTORY
Isaiah raised his hand to volunteer wholeheartedly

Don't you love it when you know the answer to a question your teacher asks? You are confident, you are eager, you are sure you know the right answer, so your hand shoots up in the air so fast! I can even see your hand waving to get your teacher's attention.

Isaiah was a prophet in the Old Testament who used to get really disgusted with people. He kept saying over and over to them, "Woe to you, woe to you, woe to you!" Then something happened to Isaiah in chapter 6. Isaiah had a vision of God and saw angels who were praising God. One of the angels flew over to Isaiah and touched his mouth with a hot coal. The angel said, "This has touched your lips. Your guilt has been taken away. Your sin has been paid for."

Today's Lectio Divina is only one verse. That's right, one verse. It's Isaiah's response to God's question. Somehow I can see his hand waving in the air after God asks the questions.

What do you think?

Scripture:

Isaiah 6: 8

Then I heard the voice of the Lord. He said, "Who will I send?" Who will go for us?" I said, "Here I am. Send me!"

S - Scripture (Read the scripture out loud slowly.)
Write the part of the scripture that stands out to you. It might be a phrase or a line or even just a word.

_____

T - Think (Read the scripture slowly again.)
Think about what the scripture is saying. How does this fit your life right now?

_____

_____

_____

_____

A - Ask (One more time...read the scripture slowly.)
Write a prayer about what God is showing you through the scripture.

_____

_____

_____

_____

R - Rest (Set your stopwatch for at least 2 - 5 minutes.)
Listen for God's still small voice (in your mind) saying who He is.
Finish this sentence, "God is my _____."

T - Tell
Tell an adult about what God has told you AND/OR you could jump online at mystartjournal.com and let us know what you learned today.

ANY STARGAZERS AMONG US?
Creation itself is on an adventure

The other night, when I was staring at the Milky Way, I thought about the stars being on an amazing adventure. The Bible talks about the morning stars singing together, the trees of the field clapping their hands, and even the mountains singing!

Did you know each star was placed in a precise spot by the Hand of God? When God put the stars in place it was like He gave us a big bouquet of star flowers. Sometimes I even wonder if God whistled when He put the stars in place. The beautiful stars at night show us we have a happy God. I know a sailor and he has sailed the Atlantic Ocean only using the stars to guide him. His name is Captain Dan. If it's cloudy, he has a harder time, but when the skies are clear he knows exactly the route to take. You can shine too, just like the stars.

Today's Lectio Divina is about nature being on an adventure. Read the verses below very slowly and see which one is a highlight for you today.

What do you think?

Scripture:
Psalm 19:1-4
The heavens tell about the glory of God. The skies show that his hands created them. Day after day they speak about it. Night after night they make it known. But they don't speak or use words. No sound is heard from them. At the same time, their voice goes out into the whole earth. Their words go out from one end of the world to the other. God has set up a tent in the heavens for the sun.

S - Scripture (Read the scripture out loud slowly.)
Write the part of the scripture that stands out to you. It might be a phrase or a line or even just a word.

_____

T - Think (Read the scripture slowly again.)
Think about what the scripture is saying. How does this fit your life right now?

_____

_____

_____

_____

A - Ask (One more time...read the scripture slowly.)
Write a prayer about what God is showing you through the scripture.

_____

_____

_____

_____

R - Rest (Set your stopwatch for at least 2 - 5 minutes.)
Listen for God's still small voice (in your mind) saying who He is.
Finish this sentence, "God is my _____."

T - Tell
Tell an adult about what God has told you AND/OR you could jump online at mystartjournal.com and let us know what you learned today.

TIME FOR A HEART CHECK-UP

"God, see what is in my heart. Know what is there. Test me. Know what I'm thinking."
Psalm 139:23

Now is the time to reflect on your journey and do a HEART CHECK-UP.

Use the three questions below to guide three prayer conversations with God.

Dear God ...

1. During the last quarter, what did I learn about You and about myself?

2. What were You highlighting to me from this quarter on Identity?

3. What action steps would You like me to take?

WEEK 39

1.

2.

3.

TRUST

MY SAFETY

Penny's Short Stories- TRUST

I love the feeling of a new school year. Freshly sharpened pencils, empty pages and a chance at a fresh start. We're about to spend the next quarter, looking at TRUST and what God says about who we are to trust and what it looks like when we trust Him. But before we do, I thought you might like to meet one of my students and hear his story.

Hey there,

I'm Dylan.

My dad's in the Navy and we move around quite a bit. I love that my dad is in the Navy. Our family loves the water and snorkelling in the ocean. But being a Navy Kid, means sometimes my dad is gone or we have to move every couple of years. I've kind of gotten used to travelling to different places by now. But having to pack up my stuff into boxes and leave my friends behind doesn't get easier. The feeling of saying goodbye is hard. I can be a little shy at times, so making friends can be tricky. Trusting people can be even harder.

My parents had been really praying for me and my little sister to settle into our new place. I was 10yrs. old at the time and really angry that we had to move again for the third time. That's when I met Miss Penny.

School started okay, but I didn't want to be the "new kid". I wanted to be the "old kid". Learning new routines and meeting new people was hard. It seemed so unfair. Because I was upset, I chose not to trust anyone. My parents would tell me to "lean on Jesus", but I didn't really understand how I could "lean" on someone I couldn't see. Anyway, could I really trust Jesus? So I took my frustration out on everyone, especially my family. School started okay, but I was MAD. I stuck to myself at recess and lunch, and sat by myself on the bus on the way home from school. I wasn't going to make friends to then have to say goodbye.

One day in one of our lessons, Miss Penny talked to us about trust. She put a chair in the middle of the room and said, "who would like to sit on this chair?" Everyone put their hand up and she pointed to one of the girls to sit in the chair. She asked the girl an interesting question, "How did you know the chair would hold you up?". The girl thought for a while and then said, "mmm...I knew it would hold me up, because I saw Antonio sitting on the chair yesterday." A grin came across Miss Penny's face, "What a great answer, Christy. Sometimes when we don't know if we can trust God, we can look and see others we know and love, who have put their trust in Him. And we know that if God can handle their problems, then He can handle ours. God wants us to lean on Him and trust Him with our lives. He is strong enough to guide us on the best pathway."

When Miss Penny said that, I remembered when my mom was saying goodbye to her friends at the Naval base. She was crying and upset, but said she trusted God would help her find new friends and she knew she could still speak to her friends on the phone. Suddenly I realized, If my mom could trust God, and lean on Him when she was upset, I could to. That day, something really changed for me. I started to understand the Proverb that tells us to trust in the Lord with all of your heart. If I could trust that God knows all about my family and friends and has a great life planned, then I would look for the good that He has planned and enjoy my life, no matter what!

Honestly, I still don't like saying goodbye. But now, I have a different perspective. I'm not just saying goodbye; I get to say HELLO to a whole new bunch of friends. Knowing I can trust God with my life and with my family, gives me peace in my heart. I'm not worried all the time or anxious about "what's coming next". So, next time you are worried about something, remember YOU CAN LEAN ON JESUS!

Dylan

You have a story, just like Dylan does. God is writing the pages of your life and creating pathways for you to live a great life. All you have to do is CHOOSE to trust God, to lean on Him. Who knows, maybe people will look at your life and see that God has been faithful to you, and be encouraged that they can put their trust in God, too!

EVERY DAY SOMEONE IS MOVING
Trusting God when you don't know where you're going

When I was in sixth grade my parents told me our family was moving to another state. No way! I wasn't moving. I was staying with my friends. Obviously they would not let me do that and the whole family moved, including me.

Some of you know what it's like to move and make new friends, like Dylan. And some of you have gone to the same school with the same friends all your life.

Jesus seemed to find people who were alone, afraid, or who needed to talk to someone. He had this special way of knowing someone's heart. My neighbor, Ezekiel, who is in 6th grade, told me that he looks for friends at his school who are sitting alone at lunch time and asks if he can eat with them. When I asked him why he did that he said God gave him the idea. I am so proud of him!

Wouldn't it be great if the next day at school all our Lectio Divina friends would look for someone who is eating alone and sit with him or her? Wow! You could start a club called the "No One Sits Alone Club!" Whether you are moving or you know someone who has just moved into your neighborhood, God wants you to trust Him as you make new friends.

Scripture:

Genesis 12:1-4

The Lord had said to Abram, "Leave your country and your people. Leave your father's family. Go to the land I will show you. I will make you into a great nation. I will bless you. I will make your name great. You will be a blessing to others. I will bless those who bless you. I will put a curse on anyone who calls down a curse on you. All nations on earth will be blessed because of you." So Abram left, just as the Lord had told him. Lot went with him. Abram was 75 years old when he left Haran.

S - Scripture (Read the scripture out loud slowly.)
Write the part of the scripture that stands out to you. It might be a phrase or a line or even just a word.

_____

T - Think (Read the scripture slowly again.)
Think about what the scripture is saying. How does this fit your life right now?

_____

_____

_____

_____

A - Ask (One more time...read the scripture slowly.)
Write a prayer about what God is showing you through the scripture.

_____

_____

_____

_____

R - Rest (Set your stopwatch for at least 2 - 5 minutes.)
Listen for God's still small voice (in your mind) saying who He is.
Finish this sentence, "God is my _____."

T - Tell
Tell an adult about what God has told you AND/OR you could jump online at mystartjournal.com and let us know what you learned today.

GOD SHOWS UP IN UNEXPECTED PLACES
Knowing who we are anywhere

A very bad thing happened to my friend's cousin, Joe. He went to prison and was charged for a big robbery that he did not commit. It was awful! My friend went to visit him every week and knew Joe was really mad! The food was bad! The bed was hard! The prisoners were mean!

Who would possibly expect God to show up there? But He did and turned my friend's cousin's heart around. His first step was to ask God to forgive him for blaming Him. It wasn't God's fault, but he thought it was. The most amazing thing happened in his heart after he asked for forgiveness. He started being friends with some of the inmates. They told him about their awful lives and my friend's cousin told them about forgiveness and the love of God. He discovered that God loves to show up in unexpected places because He loves people! God gave my friend's cousin an identity of being a Jesus-lover in that prison.

Is there something you need to ask forgiveness for? Today is a great day to read the following verses and choose to live with a clean heart.

Scripture:
1 John 1:9-10
But God is faithful and fair. If we admit that we have sinned, he will forgive us our sins. He will forgive every wrong thing we have done. He will make us pure. If we say we have not sinned, we are calling God a liar. His word has no place in our lives.

S - Scripture (Read the scripture out loud slowly.)
Write the part of the scripture that stands out to you. It might be a phrase or a line or even just a word.

_____

T - Think (Read the scripture slowly again.)
Think about what the scripture is saying. How does this fit your life right now?

_____

_____

_____

_____

A - Ask (One more time...read the scripture slowly.)
Write a prayer about what God is showing you through the scripture.

_____

_____

_____

_____

R - Rest (Set your stopwatch for at least 2 - 5 minutes.)
Listen for God's still small voice (in your mind) saying who He is.
Finish this sentence, "God is my _____."

T - Tell
Tell an adult about what God has told you AND/OR you could jump online at mystartjournal.com and let us know what you learned today.

IT'S OKAY TO CRY
Your tears have a purpose

Really! It is okay to cry! Have you ever tried to push tears back after they started running down your cheeks? Impossible! You just can't do it. God made tears to flow. He values all kinds of tears. Did you know you produce 295 milliliters (ten ounces) of tears a day and 113 liters (30 gallons) a year? Wow! Why so many? Glad you asked.

Here they are:

- Basal tears are always in your eyes to keep them lubricated

- Reflex tears protect your eyes from wind, smoke, even raw onions that your mom or dad chops.

- Emotion tears flow when you are sad or happy and calm the iris in your eyes.

You are not being a "baby" when you cry. Trust God that He made your tears for a purpose.

Today, you will read about Jesus' tears. Our story picks up when he met Mary and heard that her brother, Lazarus, who was his good friend, had died.

Scripture:
John 11: 32-36
Mary reached the place where Jesus was. When she saw him, she fell at his feet. She said, "Lord, I wish you had been here! Then my brother would not have died." Jesus saw her crying. He saw that the Jews who had come along with her were crying also. His spirit became very sad, and he was troubled. "Where have you put him?" he asked. "Come and see, Lord," they replied. Jesus sobbed. Then the Jews said, "See how much he loved him!"

S - Scripture (Read the scripture out loud slowly.)
Write the part of the scripture that stands out to you. It might be a phrase or a line or even just a word.

_____

T - Think (Read the scripture slowly again.)
Think about what the scripture is saying. How does this fit your life right now?

_____

_____

_____

_____

A - Ask (One more time...read the scripture slowly.)
Write a prayer about what God is showing you through the scripture.

_____

_____

_____

_____

R - Rest (Set your stopwatch for at least 2 - 5 minutes.)
Listen for God's still small voice (in your mind) saying who He is.
Finish this sentence, "God is my _____."

T - Tell
Tell an adult about what God has told you AND/OR you could jump online at mystartjournal.com and let us know what you learned today.

TRUSTING GOD WHEN YOU ARE AFRAID
Angels do watch over us

My brother and his family live in an unsafe neighborhood. Many nights they hear gunshots and get scared. God lives everywhere and He lives in unsafe places. Maybe you get scared at night where you live. God said He will command angels to watch over you

God commanded an angel to watch over a little baby over 3500 years ago. The children of Israel were slaves in Egypt. They were all afraid of their cruel taskmasters who worked them really hard. The Pharaoh at that time was very mean and he would command the workers who served him to be mean, really mean to the Israelites. Everyone was afraid of them, especially when they were killing their baby boys. Oh, that makes me cry!

A young Hebrew mommy named Jochebed, had a sweet baby boy and she put him in a basket by the edge of the Nile River. She trusted God to protect him. The baby's older sister kept her eye on the basket. See what happens next. The ending to this story is amazing!

We pick up the story just as Pharaoh's daughter hears a babies cry and sees a basket in the tall grass.
As she walked with her servants along the river, she asks them to go and get the basket.

Scripture:
Exodus 2:6-10
When she opened it, she saw the baby. He was crying. She felt sorry for him. "This is one of the Hebrew babies," she said. Then his sister spoke to Pharaoh's daughter. She asked, "Do you want me to go and get one of the Hebrew women? She could nurse the baby for you." "Yes, go," she answered. So the girl went and got the baby's mother. Pharaoh's daughter said to her, "Take this baby. Nurse him for me. I'll pay you." So the woman took the baby and nursed him. When the child grew older, she took him to Pharaoh's daughter. And he became her son. She named him Moses. She said, "I pulled him out of the water."

S - Scripture (Read the scripture out loud slowly.)
Write the part of the scripture that stands out to you. It might be a phrase
or a line or even just a word.

_____

T - Think (Read the scripture slowly again.)
Think about what the scripture is saying. How does this fit your life right now?

_____

_____

_____

_____

A - Ask (One more time...read the scripture slowly.)
Write a prayer about what God is showing you through the scripture.

_____

_____

_____

_____

R - Rest (Set your stopwatch for at least 2 - 5 minutes.)
Listen for God's still small voice (in your mind) saying who He is.
Finish this sentence, "God is my _____."

T - Tell
Tell an adult about what God has told you AND/OR you could jump online at
mystartjournal.com and let us know what you learned today.

GOD WORKS IN SCARY PLACES
God is greater than anything you face

Oh, my Lectio Friends, I have to tell you my zoo story. When I was visiting the zoo, a lion escaped and everyone was immediately evacuated. People were scared silly and running into each other trying to get out. I heard later the lion was found in the elephants' yard having a good time! I guess he found some friends.

Lions are ferocious! They are not big, oversized, snuggly, kitty cats and that leads into a true story of TRUST in God in a big way. The main character is Daniel, who was assigned an enormous job in Babylon with 32 other leaders. Big job! Big problem! Daniel was an Israelite, and the other 31 leaders were Babylonians, who hated him and tricked the King to announce that everyone in his kingdom should bow to the King.

Daniel loved God and would only bow down to the one true God. The wicked leaders tricked the king to declare that anyone who did not bow to him would be thrown into the lions' den. Daniel loved God only and yes, was thrown to the hungry lions. That night the king could not sleep and you will read below what happened when he checked in on Daniel the next morning.

Scripture:
Daniel 6:20-23

As he came near to the den where Daniel was, he cried out in a tone of anguish. The king declared to Daniel, "O Daniel, servant of the living God, has your God, whom you serve continually, been able to deliver you from the lions?" Then Daniel said to the king, "O King, live forever! My God sent his angel and shut the lions' mouths, and they have not harmed me, because I was found blameless before him, and also before you. O King, I have done no harm." Then the king was exceedingly glad, and commanded that Daniel be taken up out of the den. So Daniel was taken up out of the den, and no kind of harm was found on him, because he had trusted in God.

WEEK 44

S - Scripture (Read the scripture out loud slowly.)
Write the part of the scripture that stands out to you. It might be a phrase or a line or even just a word.

_____

T - Think (Read the scripture slowly again.)
Think about what the scripture is saying. How does this fit your life right now?

_____

_____

_____

_____

A - Ask (One more time...read the scripture slowly.)
Write a prayer about what God is showing you through the scripture.

_____

_____

_____

_____

R - Rest (Set your stopwatch for at least 2 - 5 minutes.)
Listen for God's still small voice (in your mind) saying who He is.
Finish this sentence, "God is my _____."

T - Tell
Tell an adult about what God has told you AND/OR you could jump online at mystartjournal.com and let us know what you learned today.

TAKE A DEEP BREATH
Trusting God with the things I need

Have you ever had stomach aches, headaches, or felt super tired because you were upset about something? Often when this happens, someone who cares about us will say something like, "Are you anxious or worried about something? Take a few deep breaths and let's talk about it." So go ahead...yeah, right now... take five big...long...deep...breaths.

Jesus says a lot about worry and anxiety in Matthew 6. He talks about not worrying about what we wear, what we eat, or anything else that keeps us from trusting Him.

Be prepared. God may just take a big worry off your mind while you experience this Lectio Divina!

Scripture:
Matthew 6:31-34
"So don't worry. Don't say, 'What will we eat?' Or, 'What will we wear?' People who are ungodly run after all of those things. Your Father who is in heaven knows that you need them. But put God's kingdom first. Do what he wants you to do. Then all of those things will also be given to you. So don't worry about tomorrow. Tomorrow will worry about itself. Each day has enough trouble of its own."

S - Scripture (Read the scripture out loud slowly.)
Write the part of the scripture that stands out to you. It might be a phrase or a line or even just a word.

_____

T - Think (Read the scripture slowly again.)
Think about what the scripture is saying. How does this fit your life right now?

_____

_____

_____

_____

A - Ask (One more time...read the scripture slowly.)
Write a prayer about what God is showing you through the scripture.

_____

_____

_____

_____

R - Rest (Set your stopwatch for at least 2 - 5 minutes.)
Listen for God's still small voice (in your mind) saying who He is.
Finish this sentence, "God is my _____."

T - Tell
Tell an adult about what God has told you AND/OR you could jump online at mystartjournal.com and let us know what you learned today.

BABY STEPS
One step at a time

Do you remember when you first started to walk? Probably not, but perhaps you heard some stories about how you took a step, then fell down, took more steps, and fell again, and then took a bunch of steps and kept going. That's what trusting God is like, taking baby steps, then bigger steps and long jumps!

You will discover today some steps to take on your personal "trust journey with God".

Scripture:

Proverbs 3:5-7

Trust in the Lord with all your heart. Do not depend on your own understanding. In all your ways remember him. Then he will make your paths smooth and straight. Don't be wise in your own eyes. Have respect for the Lord and avoid evil. That will bring health to your body. It will make your bones strong.

S - Scripture (Read the scripture out loud slowly.)
Write the part of the scripture that stands out to you. It might be a phrase or a line or even just a word.

_____

T - Think (Read the scripture slowly again.)
Think about what the scripture is saying. How does this fit your life right now?

_____

_____

_____

_____

A - Ask (One more time...read the scripture slowly.)
Write a prayer about what God is showing you through the scripture.

_____

_____

_____

_____

R - Rest (Set your stopwatch for at least 2 - 5 minutes.)
Listen for God's still small voice (in your mind) saying who He is.
Finish this sentence, "God is my _____."

T - Tell
Tell an adult about what God has told you AND/OR you could jump online at mystartjournal.com and let us know what you learned today.

HOW A LITTLE TURNED INTO A LOT
Complaining doesn't get us anywhere

It's so easy to complain, complain, complain! Complaining never gets us anywhere. We complain about how little we have, rather than seeing what God can do with a little bit of something. Wait till you hear about a widow in 2 Kings 4. Her husband died. He loved God, but when he died he owed money to someone. The poor widow did not have the money, so that person was taking her two sons to be his slaves. How sad is that?

Elisha, the prophet, showed up and asked her what she had in her home. "I have nothing, only a tiny bit of olive oil", she said hopelessly. Elisha told her to ask her neighbors for jars, many jars, and when she collected them she was to go inside her home with her sons and fill the jars up with oil from the little oil she had.

Let's see what happened and what God is saying to you about 'trust' today.

Scripture:

2 Kings 4:5-7

The woman left him. After that, she shut the door behind her and her sons. They brought the jars to her. And she kept pouring. When all of the jars were full, she spoke to one of her sons. She said, "Bring me another jar." But he replied, "There aren't any more left." Then the oil stopped flowing. She went and told the man of God about it. He said, "Go and sell the oil. Pay what you owe. You and your sons can live on what is left."

S - Scripture (Read the scripture out loud slowly.)
Write the part of the scripture that stands out to you. It might be a phrase or a line or even just a word.

_____

T - Think (Read the scripture slowly again.)
Think about what the scripture is saying. How does this fit your life right now?

_____

_____

_____

_____

A - Ask (One more time...read the scripture slowly.)
Write a prayer about what God is showing you through the scripture.

_____

_____

_____

_____

R - Rest (Set your stopwatch for at least 2 - 5 minutes.)
Listen for God's still small voice (in your mind) saying who He is.
Finish this sentence, "God is my _____."

T - Tell
Tell an adult about what God has told you AND/OR you could jump online at mystartjournal.com and let us know what you learned today.

A CAMPING ADVENTURE
Trust the promises of God

Today's trust adventure takes you on a camping trip with Jacob. Let's just pretend we are gathering our supplies...tent, sleeping bag, bug spray, food, marshmallows and more for s'mores around the campfire, etc. Everything is packed, but when you arrived at the campsite you discover you forgot your pillow and one of your friends laughingly says, "Here's a rock you can use for your pillow!" Not too funny!

In Genesis 28, Jacob did use a rock for his pillow. He even fell asleep on it! While he was asleep he had a dream about a ladder that reached from heaven to earth and angels were ascending and descending on that ladder. The Lord stood above the ladder and said, "I am the LORD, the God of Abraham your father and the God of Isaac. I will give you the land where you are sleeping and you and your children will be blessed."

Jacob woke up the next morning and poured oil on his rock pillow and called that campsite, "Bethel". Bethel means 'House of God'. Wow! What a camping trip! Find out today what else Jacob said about his dream and see what God speaks to you. How can God turn a hard rock into a promise?

Scripture:
Genesis 28:20-22
Then Jacob made a vow saying, "If God will be with me and will keep me in this way that I go and will give me bread to eat and clothing to wear, so that I come again to my father's house in peace, then the Lord shall be my God. And this stone, which I have set up for a pillar, shall be God's house. And of all that you give me I will give a full tenth to you."

WEEK 48

S - Scripture (Read the scripture out loud slowly.)
Write the part of the scripture that stands out to you. It might be a phrase or a line or even just a word.

_____

T - Think (Read the scripture slowly again.)
Think about what the scripture is saying. How does this fit your life right now?

_____

_____

_____

_____

A - Ask (One more time...read the scripture slowly.)
Write a prayer about what God is showing you through the scripture.

_____

_____

_____

_____

R - Rest (Set your stopwatch for at least 2 - 5 minutes.)
Listen for God's still small voice (in your mind) saying who He is.
Finish this sentence, "God is my _____."

T - Tell
Tell an adult about what God has told you AND/OR you could jump online at mystartjournal.com and let us know what you learned today.

DOES JESUS REALLY PRAY FOR ME?
Trust that Jesus cares so much

Sometimes adults can get busy and don't always have time to listen to us at the moment we come to them. But God isn't like that. He always has time for His kids and likes it when we talk to Him and when we take time to listen to Him. His son Jesus, talks to Him all the time. But here is something even more amazing! Did you know that Jesus is talking to God about you? About the things you and your family are facing?

When Jesus left the earth and went to heaven, He didn't go to relax and have a break from helping people. He knew that we'd need help, so He sent the Holy Spirit to come alongside us and into our lives. But Jesus didn't stop there. The Scriptures tell us that Jesus sits at the right hand of God and PRAYS FOR US. Right now, He is praying for you. He knows the concerns of your heart, where you live, what makes you scared, what you worry about and all the details of your life.

You are not alone. Today, you can trust God cares for you and is praying for you. Your friend Jesus is going to bat for you today, now that's something to be thankful for!

Scripture:
Romans 8:34
Christ Jesus is at the right hand of God and is also praying for us.

WEEK 49

S - Scripture (Read the scripture out loud slowly.)
Write the part of the scripture that stands out to you. It might be a phrase or a line or even just a word.

_____

T - Think (Read the scripture slowly again.)
Think about what the scripture is saying. How does this fit your life right now?

_____

_____

_____

_____

A - Ask (One more time...read the scripture slowly.)
Write a prayer about what God is showing you through the scripture.

_____

_____

_____

_____

R - Rest (Set your stopwatch for at least 2 - 5 minutes.)
Listen for God's still small voice (in your mind) saying who He is.
Finish this sentence, "God is my _____."

T - Tell
Tell an adult about what God has told you AND/OR you could jump online at mystartjournal.com and let us know what you learned today.

GOD MADE ME TO BE BRAVE
He is always with me

I was a fifth grade teacher for four years. I loved teaching kids and seeing them grow and learn. I remember all my students, especially Barry. He won my heart. On many days I noticed Barry didn't eat his lunch because he said he had stomach aches. He stayed in often from recess with a headache or other problems. A couple weeks passed and I knew I had to talk with Barry and his mom to to see what the problem was and how I might help him.

What we discovered still makes me very sad. There was a 6th grade boy, RJ, who every morning made fun of Barry and took his lunch money. He said if Barry gave him his money he would be his friend and because Barry wanted his friendship he gave him money every day. Some days Barry would ask his mom for more money to give to RJ, but instead of being friends, RJ called Barry bad names and threatened to beat him up if he didn't get him the money. This was a definitely a bullying situation.

Because Barry was scared of getting beat up, he isolated himself from everyone, including his friends. Here is a statistic I found: if 100 children are together and they all see somebody being bullied, 89 of them would do nothing, because bullies scare all of them. But if they get together, 2, 3 or more, and report it to an adult, something can be done. A student who is being bullied needs a friend like you and your friends to tell. Our school counselor said when friends tell, more kids feel safe.

Did you know Goliath bullied David and God gave him supernatural strength to beat Goliath? And Saul in the New Testament bullied the Christians until Jesus stepped in and stopped him in a vision. I am praying for you, your school and neighborhood. God designed you to be strong and courageous. He has given you and your friends special gifts. No bully can take those away!

Scripture:

Joshua 1:7

"Be strong and very brave. Make sure you obey the whole law my servant Moses gave you. Do not turn away from it to the right or the left. Then you will have success everywhere you go.

S - Scripture (Read the scripture out loud slowly.)
Write the part of the scripture that stands out to you. It might be a phrase or a line or even just a word.

_____

T - Think (Read the scripture slowly again.)
Think about what the scripture is saying. How does this fit your life right now?

_____

_____

_____

_____

A - Ask (One more time...read the scripture slowly.)
Write a prayer about what God is showing you through the scripture.

_____

_____

_____

_____

R - Rest (Set your stopwatch for at least 2 - 5 minutes.)
Listen for God's still small voice (in your mind) saying who He is.
Finish this sentence, "God is my _____."

T - Tell
Tell an adult about what God has told you AND/OR you could jump online at mystartjournal.com and let us know what you learned today.

GOD SEES ME
Trust that God knows me

I was teaching a class one day, and one of my students got upset with another classmate and ran away. I watched him run and hide in the sandpit at the back of the school. I knew where he was, but he thought I couldn't see him. When our eyes finally locked on each other, and he knew I saw him, we started talking and he came back to class.

It reminds me of a Bible character called Hagar. You can find her story in Genesis 16. She was mistreated by her boss and was so upset she ran away. Have you ever felt like that? Sometimes things can feel overwhelming and we're not too sure how to cope with them. But in the hot desert, an angel found her and told her what God wanted her to do. At the end of the conversation, Hagar said, "You are the God who sees me." He saw her trouble and cared enough to send someone to tell her what God wanted to say.

It's the same for you and for me.

God sees us and he wants to talk with us. Let Him talk to you today as you reflect on the psalmist's words in Psalm 139.

Scripture:
Psalm 139:1-2
Lord, you have seen what is in my heart. You know all about me. You know when I sit down and when I get up. You know what I'm thinking even though you are far away.

S - Scripture (Read the scripture out loud slowly.)
Write the part of the scripture that stands out to you. It might be a phrase or a line or even just a word.

_____

T - Think (Read the scripture slowly again.)
Think about what the scripture is saying. How does this fit your life right now?

_____

_____

_____

_____

A - Ask (One more time...read the scripture slowly.)
Write a prayer about what God is showing you through the scripture.

_____

_____

_____

_____

R - Rest (Set your stopwatch for at least 2 - 5 minutes.)
Listen for God's still small voice (in your mind) saying who He is.
Finish this sentence, "God is my _____."

T - Tell
Tell an adult about what God has told you AND/OR you could jump online at mystartjournal.com and let us know what you learned today.

TIME FOR A HEART CHECK-UP

"God, see what is in my heart. Know what is there. Test me. Know what I'm thinking."
Psalm 139:23

Now is the time to reflect on your journey and do a HEART CHECK-UP.

Use the three questions below to guide three prayer conversations with God.

Dear God ...

1. During the last quarter, what did I learn about You and about myself?

2. What were You highlighting to me from this quarter on Identity?

3. What action steps would You like me to take?

WEEK 52

1.

2.

3.

The MYSTART adventure is about saying YES to Jesus

Throughout our Lectio journey together, we have had the opportunity to learn about God, discovering more about His plan for our lives from the Bible. The problem is that people have rejected God's best plan for their lives.

WHAT'S THE PROBLEM?

God made us so that we would be close friends with Him forever, but ever since Adam and Eve, people have chosen to go their own way, forgetting about Him. This created a big gap between people and God. Some people realized the gap that existed, and tried to be good to get to heaven. But the truth is, we could never be good enough to come to God.

So, God had to make a plan so we could join his family.

GOD'S BIG PLAN:

- God rescued THE WORLD. He sent His son, Jesus to the earth to show His great love to us. Jesus was without sin and didn't deserve to die, but He took the punishment for our sin when He died on the cross, and rose again on the third day to show His mighty power.
- God's hope is that people everywhere will hear about His son and all He has done and turn from their own ways and turn to Jesus. Putting their trust in God.
- God gave us peace with Him and a fresh start.
- The new start they make with Jesus is the beginning of a LIFELONG friendship that will never end. Kids can be sure, that when they say YES to Jesus, they don't need to be afraid of dying. Jesus is the friend that lasts for all eternity. He plans our days and is preparing a place in heaven for those who know Him.

HOW DO I SAY YES TO JESUS?

1. Say this prayer out loud:

Dear God, I know that I am a sinner. I know that you sent Jesus to be my Savior, and that He died on the cross to take the punishment for my sins. I know that Jesus rose from the dead and is coming back someday. Please forgive me of all of my sins, and come into my life and change me. Please guide me in my life and help me to follow you. Thank you for saving me and taking me to heaven when I die. In Jesus' Name, Amen.

2. **Welcome to the Family! Go and tell** an adult, you could even go online to www.mystartjournal.com and tell us. We'd love to hear from you!

Scripture References: John 3:16, Romans 3:23, Romans 6:23 and Romans 10:9.

ABOUT THE AUTHORS

HARRIET Z. MOUER

Where you live: Amherst, Ohio - USA
Year you married Bill: 1967
Kids/grandkids: 3 married children, 7 grandchildren
Jobs you've had: Music/Piano Teacher, Gift Basket Designer, Children's/Women's Pastor, District Supervisor (Foursquare Church), Lifeforming Leadership Coach
Hobbies: Bike riding, Walking, Playing Piano, laughing with my grandchildren
Hot drink you love: White Pomegranate Tea
Favourite Christmas Movie: Miracle on 34th Street
Fun games you like to play: Farkle, Apples to Apples
Life verse: John 10:10
Bible character that inspires you: Priscilla

REBECCA A. TOBAR

Nickname: Bec
Where you live: Sydney, Australia
Year you married Cristian: 1998
Kids: I have 3 kids - Caleb (13), Silas (8), Ella (6)
Jobs you've had: Elementary School Teacher, Youth/Kids/Creative Pastor/Executive Pastor at HopePoint Church
Instruments you play: Piano, Guitar
Sports you love: Softball, Hockey, Basketball
Hot drink you love: Mocha
Favourite Christmas movie: White Christmas
Fun games you like to play: Karaoke, Spotlight
Life verse: Ephesians 3:20
Bible character that inspires you: Deborah

GRAPHIC DESIGN
REBECCA S. SCHOFIELD

Beck is a Graphic Designer, Elementary School Teacher and Pastor in Sydney, Australia. She has two beautiful children; Willow and Harvey, with her husband Grant. She loves seeing kids discover their God-given uniqueness.

CPSIA information can be obtained
at www.ICGtesting.com
Printed in the USA
FFOW02n0023100118
44453112-44253FF